STAND AND
DELIVER

Also available from Dale Carnegie Training

Leadership Mastery

The 5 Essential People Skills

Make Yourself Unforgettable

STAND AND DELIVER

How to Become a Masterful Communicator and Public Speaker

DALE CARNEGIE TRAINING

**SIMON &
SCHUSTER**

London · New York · Sydney · Toronto

A CBS COMPANY

First published in Great Britain by Simon & Schuster UK Ltd, 2011
A CBS COMPANY

Copyright © 2011, by Dale Carnegie & Associates, Inc.

1 3 5 7 9 10 8 6 4 2

Simon & Schuster UK Ltd
1st Floor
222 Gray's Inn Road
London
WC1X 8HB

www.simonandschuster.co.uk

Simon & Schuster Australia
Sydney

A CIP catalogue for this book is available
from the British Library.

ISBN: 978-0-85720-676-3

Printed in the UK by CPI Cox & Wyman, Reading, Berkshire RG1 8EX

Contents

Introduction

Welcome to *Stand and Deliver*! You're about to begin the most complete, powerful, and *practical* book ever created on the art and science of speaking in public. Dale Carnegie Training® is the world leader in training programs for public speaking mastery, and the Nightingale-Conant Corporation is the world's leading producer of audio learning technology. In *Stand and Deliver*, Dale Carnegie and Nightingale-Conant give you the tools you need to become an outstanding public speaker in the shortest possible time. You'll learn how to prepare and organize a talk, whether it's five minutes in front of a small group or half an hour before a packed auditorium. You'll discover the real keys not just for entertaining your listeners, but for informing them, persuading them, and *inspiring* them to action based on your message. Perhaps most important, *Stand and Deliver* will show you how to take the fear out of oral presentation once and for all.

Before you begin, a quick overview of the book's organization will be helpful. *Stand and Deliver* comprises twelve chapters, each focused on a different and important principle of public speaking. The only exceptions to this are chapters 8 and 9, both of which are devoted to the concept of persuasion.

Interposed among the chapters are a number of insightful quotes dealing with public speaking. Some of these are from ancient times, while others are much more recent. But they all pertain to the material covered in the book, and they all shed light on fundamental issues that every public speaker faces.

In addition, you will also find "case studies," focusing on acknowledged masters of the public speaker's art. These sub-chapters include selections from the most effective presentations of each speaker. Since you aspire to be a master speaker yourself, it's a good idea to read these selections carefully. Notice how some of them seem formal and dignified, while others are more relaxed and contemporary. But all of them convey the sense of confidence and control that is the hallmark of a master speaker. There are many paths to this goal, but each path leads to a profound connection with the audience. That connection leads listeners not only to thought and feeling, but to action as well.

Finally, in creating this book we faced a unique challenge. Many aspects of life in the twenty-first century are more highly developed than ever before. Our athletes are better, our computers are faster, and our life expectancy has increased. But let's be honest: with a few exceptions, great public speakers—or even competent ones—are now few and far between. Partly for that reason, and also to prevent the book from becoming dated by personalities who will not stand the test of time, *Stand and Deliver* frequently draws on incidents and personalities from the not-too-recent past. True, events such as the first Kennedy-Nixon debate have been discussed before. But it would be a mistake to turn away from one of the all-time best examples of public speaking issues just for the sake of the calendar.

Right now, you may see public speaking as a danger to be avoided or a challenge to be overcome. But make no mistake:

when you reach the end of this program, you'll know that speaking in public is an opportunity to be fully and joyfully embraced. You'll look forward to speaking whenever the occasion arises, and your ability to express yourself sincerely and forcefully will be a major asset in your career. All that and more awaits you in *Stand and Deliver*.

CHAPTER 1

Keys to High Impact Delivery

The Dale Carnegie organization is the world's leading resource for public speaking mastery, and this has been true for almost a century. Just as certainly, the Nightingale-Conant Corporation is the world leader in audio learning technology. Now, Dale Carnegie and Nightingale-Conant are proud to bring you this definitive book on speaking in public. So whether you're just starting out, or if you already have extensive experience with oral presentations, *Stand and Deliver* will take you to the next level of mastery.

Literally since the dawn of civilization, speaking well in front of others has been an ongoing human challenge. This was especially true for the classical civilizations of Greece and Rome, but public speaking ability was also highly esteemed in biblical times, and by Native American tribes, and by the cultures of India and China. Fascinating as it might be, however, our purpose here is not a history lesson. So right at the outset, we're going to introduce three key tools for creating a high impact presentation. These are timeless principles upon which all great speakers have relied—though each has done so in his or her own way. By blending your unique identity with the universal principles we're about to discuss, you can transform yourself into an effective public speaker almost instantly. So please read carefully. What you're about to learn will have a dramatic effect not only on how you communicate to others, but on how you see yourself as well.

Human beings are *talking* beings. We start talking when we wake up in the morning and we keep at it until we go to sleep— and some people don't even stop then. Good conversation is one of the great joys of human commerce. Good conversation should be like the game of tennis, in which the ball is struck back and forth, with each player participating equally. Bores are like golfers who just keep hitting their own ball, over and over and over.

Good conversationalists make good speakers. They're sensitive to the presence of others. Their antennae are forever alert, picking up signals from their audience and responding to those signals in the presentation. Good speakers achieve a marvelous give-and-take with listeners, just as good conversationalists do in a social setting.

More specifically, both speakers and conversationalists recognize that people desire recognition more than any other factor. They frequently ask questions such as "Do you agree with that?" Then they'll pause and read the response that's forthcoming. It might be silence, rapt attention, nods, laughter, or concern. If listeners are bored, they will always find ways of showing that, despite their polite efforts to hide their feelings. If they're interested, they'll show that too. As speakers, we have a duty to be interesting or we shouldn't stand before an audience in the first place. Creating interest is the task of the speaker, whether we're the manager of the sales force in a car dealership, an insurance agency, a real estate office, or a large international organization. When interest leaves, the sell goes out of our message.

Our responsibility is not only to create a speech that will lead an audience to a believable conclusion. We must also make the building blocks of that conclusion as fascinating as we can. In this way we can hold the attention of our audience until we get to that all-important final point. In addition, if we can develop techniques that make our audience feel that we are conversing with them, we will convey that we care what they are thinking, and that will create the emotional climate for them to accept us as favorably as possible.

Along with understanding the similarities between speaking in conversation and speaking in public, you should also understand certain important differences. You need to master certain key skills that *create the illusion* that your presentation is as personal as a one-on-one conversation—but that illusion is only possible when you've professionalized yourself as a speaker. David Letterman has the ability to speak with virtually anybody while 10 million viewers are looking in. Yet he's able to make this seem as casual as a break at the office watercooler. Now, you many not think of David Letterman as a great public speaker, but he draws on the same principles that virtually every accomplished speaker has used since ancient times.

What are these principles? The first is actually quite obvious, and maybe that's why so many speakers seem to forget it. It can be stated in a single, short sentence: *know what you're talking about.* Learn the material so well that you own it. Don't just have some expertise in your topic—*master it.* Be able to fill every second of your presentation with solid content. Once you're able to do that, 90 percent of your work will be done before you even get up in front of the audience.

To make this point, Dale Carnegie liked to invoke the

example of Luther Burbank, a great scientist by any measure and probably the greatest botanist of all time. Burbank once said, "I have often produced a million plants in order to find one or two really good ones—and then I destroyed all the inferior specimens." A presentation ought to be prepared in that same lavish and discriminating spirit. Assemble a hundred thoughts and discard ninety—or even ninety-nine. Collect more material, more information, than there is any possibility of employing. Gather it for the additional confidence it will give you, and for the sureness of touch. Gather it for the effect it will have on your mind and heart and whole manner of speaking. This is a basic factor in preparation. Yet speakers constantly ignore it. Mr. Carnegie actually believed that speakers should know forty times more about their topic than they share in a presentation!

Knowing one topic supremely well is obviously much more practical than trying to master a larger number. Professional salespeople, marketing experts, and leaders in the advertising profession know the importance of selling one thing at a time. Only catalogs can successfully handle a multitude of items. In a five-minute speech or even a long speech, it's important to have a single theme, and like a good salesperson, you pose the problem and then give your solution. At the end, the problem is restated and the solution quickly summarized.

Your opening statement should be an attention getter. For example, you might say, "Scientists all over the world are agreed that the world's oceans are dying." A sobering thought indeed. It captures immediate interest, and everyone is thinking, "Why, that would presage the end of the world. What are we doing about it?"

By invoking an internationally recognized authority as

your reference—someone such as the late Jacques Cousteau, for instance—you provide supporting evidence that your opening remark is true, then you outline the possible ways that the disaster might be averted. At the end, you might say, "Yes, the oceans of the world are dying today, but if we can marshal the combined efforts of the world's peoples, if we can influence every maritime country to pass laws governing the pollution of the seas by oil tankers . . ." So you end on a note of hope and at the same time enlist the sympathy of every one of your listeners in your cause.

Not all talks are about social problems, of course. You might be talking about a recent fishing trip, in which case you find something of special interest in the story and open with that. You might say, "Ounce for ounce, the rainbow trout is one of the gamest fish on earth." It's a much better attention getter and interest stimulator than saying, "I want to tell you about my recent fishing trip." After a few words about the fish you were after, you can work in the rest. "Two weeks ago, John Cooper and I decided to try our luck on the White River near Carter, Arkansas. It's one of the most naturally beautiful spots in the country . . ." Stay with the trip and that rainbow trout, the hero of your story, and how good it tasted cooked over an open fire on the bank of the river. Then at the close, to more closely link your listeners to the subject, you might say, "If you've never been trout fishing, let me recommend it as one of the world's best ways to forget your problems, clear your brain, and gain a new perspective. And when you hook a rainbow trout, you're in for one of the greatest thrills of a lifetime."

Watch your personal pronouns. Keep yourself out of your conversation as much as possible. In the fishing story, talk about the fish, the beautiful scenery, your companions, other people you met, a humorous incident or two perhaps, but don't keep saying, "I did this" and "I did that." The purpose of the speech is not to talk about you but rather the subject matter.

An old saying is that small minds talk about things, average minds talk about people, and great minds talk about ideas. What you're selling is almost always an idea, even if it's painting the house. The idea is the good appearance or the protection of the house. The fishing-trip story is about the idea of getting away and going after exciting game fish. One idea, well developed, is the key.

A beautiful painting is put together by a thousand brushstrokes, each stroke making a contribution to the main theme, the overall picture. It's the same with a good speech.

When speakers—especially inexperienced speakers—prepare a talk, their biggest fear is not having enough to say to fill the allotted time. Most people worry that they'll run out of material in the middle of their talk, but they respond to this fear in a misguided way. They "puff" their presentation. They wind up trying to cram the story of their lives into their fifteen minutes at the podium. The presentation gets bigger, but instead of really growing, it just swells. This is an especially dangerous pitfall for new speakers since it's usually unconscious. The principle of knowing what you're talking about doesn't mean you have to say it all. You say just enough to fill your time effectively. You leave your audience wanting more, and if you've truly mastered your subject, they'll know that there *is* more. You'll project knowledge to them that's above and beyond your actual spoken words.

To reach this level of mastery, you should begin preparing

ten days to two weeks before your event. Start your preparation by sitting down with a pencil and paper for twenty minutes—no less and no more—and writing at least fifty questions about your topic. Fifty is the minimum, but you should definitely try for as many as possible. Write your questions as quickly as you can. Don't give them a lot of thought. That's why the twenty-minute time limit is important. This stage of preparation is a sprint, not a leisurely stroll through your mental library.

During this twenty-minute session, you're creating an outline for your talk—and we want to stress the importance of putting this in the form of questions. Research shows that this is much more stimulating to the brain than a conventional outline, and since you're not supplying answers at this point, it can also be done much faster. The answers will come later in other sessions leading up to your talk.

Let me repeat, your first session should be limited to twenty minutes, and it should be done the old-fashioned way, with an actual pencil and paper.

In your second session, you'll start supplying answers to your questions and providing evidence for your ideas. This is when the computer becomes an essential tool. Begin by creating a document file of your questions—there should be *at least* fifty—and quickly writing an answer for each one based on your own knowledge. Write this just as you would say it if you were sitting in Starbucks with a good friend. Unlike your first session, you don't have to limit yourself to twenty minutes, but don't feel as if you have to answer all of your questions either. Just keep at it until you feel your energy start to fade. Resist the temptation to use the Internet to gather information. That will come later. Right now your job is to access everything you know about your topic, which is probably a lot more than you *think* you know.

It may take you several sessions to answer all the questions you wrote down, but that's no problem as long as you begin at least ten days in advance. Just make sure that you complete your answers with three or four days left before your talk. In those final sessions, you can surf the Internet for facts and figures to enhance what you've already written. Remember, you don't have to report everything there is to know about your topic. Ideally, you have total mastery of your subject, but that's for your benefit as much as for the audience's. Mastery allows you to feel completely confident in your role as an authority. It's not something you have to demonstrate in the actual words that come out of your mouth. So pick and choose the pertinent and hard-hitting information that you want to include. Think of your talk as a special meal you're preparing in your home for some honored guests. Don't think of it as a full service restaurant.

For some presentations you have little or no prior information. Other times the opposite will be true. For example, if you're talking about your own life or career, you'll have a wealth of material on the subject. Your problem is to select and arrange the information. Don't try to tell your audience everything because it can't be done. Your talk will come off as sketchy and fragmented. On the other hand, if you're talking about something that's less familiar to you, avoid trying to cover this up with excessive research. Be frank with yourself and your audience about your relationship to the topic. You don't have to say you feel ignorant about it, but you don't have to pretend you're a total expert either. You might want to take only one aspect of your topic and expand upon it. Don't make your talk an abstraction. Make liberal use of illustrations, personal observations, and self-revelations. Think of specific situations you've observed, and let those situations reveal any general principles. Your goal should always be to share your authentic point of view with the audience. That may be the view of an excited and highly motivated learner, or of an experienced and completely genuine, reliable, and empathetic teacher. By showing this is who you really are, you'll capture the goodwill of your listeners.

So far we've learned about creating the content for your talk. Now you're probably wondering how you should organize it to fit the time you've been allotted. You're wondering how to configure all that information into a coherent presentation. If you're like most people, you're especially concerned about making sure you don't suddenly freeze up when you stand behind the microphone. Shouldn't you memorize all or part of what you're going to say? Shouldn't you at least write it out?

No, you should definitely not memorize all or part of your talk, and, no, you should not even write it out. If you do, your presentation will probably sound as if you're reading rather than speaking. Later in the book we discuss organizational templates for talks of various lengths. Those will be valuable tools, but the technique we're going to look at now is something very different. It's the technique of *rehearsal.*

Rehearsing your presentation should happen in two ways, and the first one takes place entirely inside your head. As your written preparation is continuing, you should constantly be revisiting, revising, and rehearsing your talk in your mind. That means you're going to be thinking and *re*thinking your topic for at least ten days. Think of it when you first wake up in the morning. Think of it some more just before bed. Go over it in your mind while you're eating breakfast. Go over it again if you have a commute to work. See what new ideas you can come up with, or what old ideas don't seem to be working anymore.

Think about your listeners and their expectations. Think also about your expectations of yourself. What are your goals in this presentation? Do you want to inform, inspire, entertain, persuade—or all of these? Think about the physical setting in which your talk will take place. How big will the room be? How many people will it hold, and how many will actually be present? How much influence can you have on these practical details? For example, it's best not to have a small group of people in a large room. Focusing on these issues beforehand will help ensure that your presentation achieves its purpose.

Clearly identify your subject and your purpose to yourself, then let the creative process take over. As it does, you can begin speaking your presentation aloud. The car is an ideal place to do this, but you can also try it at home while looking in a mirror. Get a feel for the timing of your words and sentences. Amend them and refine them, both for their content and for the time that they take. If you're an inexperienced speaker, estimating the time of a presentation can be deceptive. Despite the common fear of running out of things to say, most people actually have more material than they think. This is better than having too little, but it can throw off your timing. Presentations almost always take longer to deliver than you think the material will last.

But all of this is only one kind of rehearsal—rehearsing by

yourself. You should also be practicing your talk with your friends. You can ask a friend to listen to an actual run-through of your presentation, or you can just brainstorm about your topic. But make your presentation your main topic of conversation as often as you can. Pay close attention to how people react to different phrases and ideas.

As you do these live rehearsals, you'll see that a structure begins to evolve. Ideally, this will be organic, but you'll also want to consciously organize your talk in line with the templates you'll be learning later in this book. Keep in mind what experienced speakers call the rule of three. A simple application of this would mean giving your talk in three main sections. Then each section has three subsections. Depending on your time limits, each of these could then have three sections, and so on. Something about the three-part formula creates a natural flow, and you'll want to take full advantage of that.

Your rehearsals will show how important it is to have a strong opening and a strong close. As you'll learn later in this book, there are many tools for getting off to a fast start, but as a general rule you must tell people what you're going to speak about and what your purpose is. They need to feel that the talk is important to you, and they certainly need to feel it's important to them. That's your first order of business. At the close, a stirring quotation or an amazing statistic is always a good choice. Give your listeners some last thing to think and talk about. Try out different closes in your rehearsals, and ask for honest feedback about the effects.

This famous quote holds true: "Tell 'em what you're gonna tell 'em. Tell 'em. And then tell 'em what you told 'em." A presentation structured along those lines will have an opening, a middle, and a close. But you're not finished yet. Far from it. We've talked about creating content and we've begun to explore ways of structuring your presentation. Now we're going to look at delivery. Content and organization are important, but as Dale Carnegie liked to say, "Depth of conviction counts more than height of logic, and enthusiasm is worth more than knowledge."

If you've ever attended a college debate competition or listened to an argument between two teenagers, you've probably noticed one key point. By no means does the person with the facts and figures always emerge as the winner. Rather, it's the person who sounds the best. It's the person who presents an argument so well that it seems to be correct, even if not.

So let's give this aspect, delivery, some serious attention. If you've never spoken in public before, you're likely to have one particular strong feeling when you try it for the first time. If you're already an experienced speaker, still pay close attention, because you'll see the truth of it. You see, the first time you make a public presentation, you'll be using the English language just as you always do. You'll be using the same words and phrases—but you'll be talking rather than *speaking* in a professional sense. You'll be communicating information, but you won't be *delivering* it in a meaningful and powerful way.

Dale Carnegie once described a clear example of this. He was staying at a hotel in England that brought in weekly speakers for the entertainment and education of the guests. One of these speakers was a well-known British writer, and her topic was "The Future of the Novel." While she was an excellent writer, it quickly became clear that speaking was not her strong suit. She admitted right off that she had not selected the topic herself and had nothing she really cared to say about it. She'd made some rambling notes. With the notes in her hand, she stood in front of her audience ignoring them—not even looking at them, sometimes staring over their heads, sometimes at her notes, sometimes at the floor. She spoke her words into some primeval void with a faraway look in her eyes and a faraway ring in her voice.

As Dale Carnegie quickly saw, that wasn't a presentation at all, but a monologue. There was no sense of connection with the listeners, and connection is the essence of effective public speaking. The audience must feel that a message is being delivered straight from the mind and heart of the speaker to their own minds and hearts. So how exactly does that happen?

The whole art known as oratory or rhetoric is mostly useless for our purposes today. Old-fashioned oratory, in which the speaker sets off all kinds of verbal fireworks, just won't work in a contemporary setting. The modern audience—whether it's fifteen people in a conference room or a thousand people in an arena or millions watching their televisions—wants speakers to talk directly and personally. People want a public presentation to have the same intimacy as a private chat. But that's not all they want. Paradoxically, they also expect this intimate exchange to be delivered with considerable force—and that's a tall order. Somehow you have to do something that's quite unnatural and yet make it seem like the most natural thing in the world.

Some books will tell you that this is all a matter of getting in touch with your deepest emotions and your strongest feelings. While it's certainly important to care for what you're talking about, the secret to outstanding delivery is more about the mind than the heart. Creating a connection with your listeners is a rational rather than an emotional process. It may *seem* emotional, and definitely should be. But as with any form of magic, what you see is only a fraction of what's really going on.

This has always been true of any art form. Masterpieces such as Leonardo da Vinci's *Mona Lisa* or Michelangelo's *David* appear to be living beings, but they are actually based on a mathematical understanding of human form and proportion. Even stand-up comedy depends on setting up certain rhythms that are as predictable as the chiming of a clock. You can learn a great deal about effective public speaking by adopting a scientifically analytical view. Once you are confidently in control of this perspective, you'll find that the emotions will take care of themselves.

A first principle of high impact delivery is your conscious choice of which words to emphasize. The meaning of any English sentence is based on the stress placed on the words, much more so than on their dictionary definitions. It's easy to prove this. Just pick any sentence and repeat it several times, each time emphasizing different words. As you can see, the meaning changes entirely. What's more, some versions of the sentence are much more compelling and interesting than others.

You can put this rule to work in a presentation. Read this sentence aloud without giving any of the words extra stress:

"I have succeeded in whatever I have started because I have willed it. I never hesitated, which has given me an advantage over the rest of mankind."

That was uniform stress. Because none of the words were emphasized, the passions and viewpoint of the speaker weren't really communicated.

Now read it again, this time emphasizing key words.

"I have *succeeded* in whatever I have started because I have *willed* it. I *never* hesitated, which has given me an advantage over the rest of mankind."

Notice, for example, how stressing the word *never* brings drama to the sentence. The emphasis on *never* hesitating suggests that there has been a struggle against hesitation. It even implies that the struggle is still going on; if it weren't, why would there be such energy placed on the word *never?* The stress you give to certain words is where the meaning of the sentence comes from. If you stress every word the same, the meaning can diminish or even disappear. So as you rehearse your presentation, try different variations of emphasis to get exactly the effect you want.

In addition to changing the stress you give to words, you should also vary the pitch of your voice. Stress is a matter of loudness or softness, but pitch is a quality of tone. In conversation, the pitch of our voices naturally flows up and down the scale from high to low and back again. This is perfectly natural, and the effect is pleasing. Why, then, once people get in front of an audience, do their voices become so dull and monotonous? The answer is twofold. First, they're tense, or even frightened, which tends to flatten delivery. And second, they're not aware of or not in control of this happening. Once again, the solution is to make your tone a conscious choice rather than an unconscious process.

When you find yourself talking with a monotonous pitch—and it will usually be high—pause for a second and say to yourself, "I'm not speaking like I normally speak. I've lapsed into the constricted tone of an inexperienced presenter. Verbally, I need to get back to who I really am."

In addition to stress and pitch, the speed with which you talk is a hugely important. To make this point, Dale Carnegie quoted this passage from a biography of Abraham Lincoln:

"Lincoln would speak several words with great rapidity, come to the word or phrase he wished to emphasize, and let his voice linger and bear hard on that phrase. Then he would rush to the end of his sentence like lightning. He would devote as much time to the word or two he wished to emphasize as he did to half a dozen less important words following it."

So many effects can be achieved by varying the speed of your words. Suppose, for example, you were to say "thirty million dollars" fast, as if that were a trivial sum of money. It may actually be a trivial amount in some corporate boardrooms or congressional hearings. "Thirty millions dollars" is dashed off as if it were nothing. But now say, "Thirrrrttttyyyy millllionnnn dollllarrrsss," extending every syllable to the maximum. Now it seems like a lot of money. By increasing the time you took to say it, it's almost as if you've increased the amount itself. Yet the actual words you've spoken are just the same.

By now, I'm sure you're beginning to see that high impact speaking is within the reach of everyone, as long as you're aware of both the obstacles and the tools for removing them. Getting you started on that awareness has been the purpose of this first chapter, and we've covered a lot of ground. We've introduced the basics of preparation, emphasizing the power of a questions-and-answers outline to create mastery. We've mentioned the usefulness of computers and Internet research, and also the need to think independently of those technologies. We've spoken about rehearsing your presentation out loud, both with your friends and with yourself as the only listener. Finally, we've seen how technical variables such as emphasis, pitch, and speed can enhance the power and meaning of a presentation.

These are all important concepts. If you really master them all and put them to work, you can become an extremely effective public speaker even if you read no further in this book. Yet we've only scratched the surface. There's so much more to learn about public speaking—and the benefits of learning it are so great—that you'll want to move ahead as soon as possible. Remember, no one knew more about public speaking than Dale Carnegie, and nowhere will you find more of that knowledge than in the book you're reading right now.

In chapter 2, you'll see why being a high impact speaker is first and foremost about just being yourself.

There are always three speeches for every one you actually give. The one you practiced, the one you gave, and the one you wish you gave.

—Dale Carnegie

It usually takes me more than three weeks to prepare a good impromptu speech.

—Mark Twain

Be sincere; be brief; be seated.

—Franklin D. Roosevelt

CHAPTER 2

What Every Listener Really Wants.
What Every Speaker Needs to Know

A surprisingly small number of basic concepts make up the foundation of all effective speaking. One of these concepts may be the foundation of personal effectiveness in any form, and it can be expressed in just two words. They're the same two words that were engraved above the entrance to the school of philosophy in ancient Greece, and they've been the basis of all wisdom ever since. These two magic words are *know thyself.* Because, until you understand who you really are, you can't really understand the world around you. And you certainly can't be an effective public speaker.

To see what this means, let's consider the two men whose work made this book possible: Dale Carnegie and Earl Nightingale. Both men were outstanding public speakers, but they earned that distinction in different ways. Dale Carnegie grew up on a farm in Missouri. His speaking style reflected his down-to-earth Midwestern roots. Though he was obviously intelligent and well-read, he looked and sounded like a neighbor from across the road rather than a professor or a politician. This was who he was, and this was what he sounded like.

Earl Nightingale, on the other hand, was gifted with a voice like an Old Testament prophet's. For more than thirty years, his daily radio broadcasts captured the attention of millions of listeners, partly because his voice simply could not be ignored. He sounded like wisdom personified. Earl Nightingale had a completely different speaking style from Dale Carnegie's, but it worked equally well because it expressed his authentic self.

You probably understand the benefits of being your natural self when it's your turn to speak. But you may not understand who your natural self really is. That's why "knowing thyself" should begin with some clear-eyed self-appraisal. How, for example, would you describe your style of interaction with other people? Are you naturally reserved, preferring to let others take the conversational lead? Or are you more outgoing and accessible? Are you an analytic, logical thinker, or do you like to tell stories and anecdotes to get your ideas across? How would you describe your physical appearance? Are you a large, gregarious person in body and in voice? Or are you someone who doesn't immediately attract a lot of notice?

A good way to approach these questions is by identifying some well-known speakers that you admire. Dale Carnegie and Earl Nightingale were great, but partly because their speaking styles were perfectly in sync with their times. The Dale Carnegie organization is successful because it's stayed on the leading edge of learning and training techniques. You should do the same in finding your role models for public speaking. We'll be talking about Winston Churchill and Abraham Lincoln in these chapters, and we'll also be talking about Bill Clinton and Jerry Seinfeld. Which of these personalities do you want to use as the basis for your speaking style? Which of them do you *not* want to use? How can you take what you admire from one speaker and blend it with what you admire from another—with the goal of making your own style entirely unique and original?

These questions have no right or wrong answers. In responding to them, the only mistake you can make is not being frank and honest. That's the good news. The bad news is, almost *everybody* makes that mistake. You see, when people have to get up before an audience, their self-perception can be fooled by two deceptive emotions. The first is hope, and the second is fear. The second of these is certainly much more common than the first, but let's start with a look at how *expecting too much* can undermine your talk just as much as worry and anxiety.

Some people have been waiting all their lives to stand up and show the world how interesting they really are. If you're one of those people, that's great, because I have no doubt that you really are interesting. I'm certain that you have some great things to say and that people will benefit from hearing you. Nevertheless, it's still important not to take your audience for granted. Yes, they want to hear you. More important, they want to *like* you—but they also want you to earn their interest and their affection. They want you to win them over. Even while they're listening to you with rapt attention, they want to know that the focus is still *on them.* So if you just can't wait to get behind that microphone and start talking, congratulations—that's a good feeling. But you should also take a half step back to remember a key principle of all Dale Carnegie training. That is, *people's favorite subject is always themselves.* Your task is to balance your own positive and healthy self-perception with the self-interest of your audience.

Let's look at a real-life example. Former president Bill Clinton is an outstanding public speaker, and an excellent example of how to "be yourself" in front of an audience. He's especially effective in question-and-answer sessions, with an amazing combination of factual knowledge and personal connection. But he didn't start out that way by any means. At the Democratic National Convention in 1988, the young governor of Arkansas gave a keynote address that was not only long on enthusiasm— it was just plain long. Clinton was so obviously enamored of his first moments in the national spotlight that he lost track of everything else. After he'd been talking for about forty minutes, he said something like "Now, in closing . . ."—and the audience began to cheer. Some had speculated that Clinton might even have entered the '88 presidential race himself, but his keynote address showed that he needed a bit more seasoning. His eagerness to make himself heard was a good quality, but sometimes there can be too much of a good thing.

While Bill Clinton was overly eager to show the world who he was, many more public speakers are determined to show who they aren't. Their speaking personality is negatively rather than positively defined. Their first priority is to not be long-winded, to not be obscure, to not be dull—and as a result, they get themselves all tied up in "nots." One of the fundamental principles of effective public speaking is, don't apologize. That means more than not saying you're sorry. It means that you shouldn't step up to the podium with the attitude that you don't deserve to be there. It means that you shouldn't try to win the audience over by referring to your own nervousness or your unworthiness to make the speech you're about to give. You may think that your conspicuous humility will win them over, but there's also a good chance that they'll simply agree with your self-deprecation.

In public speaking as in any other area of life, discovering your true self may take a bit of time. You may alternate between an overly eager presentation, and an excessively restrained one. But keep one thing in mind: great speakers are made, not born. Developing yourself as a public speaker is a creative art, just like painting or sculpture. The only difference is, *you* are both the artist and the medium.

But that's not all. Public speaking is also a science, in which certain axioms have been proven true over time. Developing the art of public speaking may involve some trial and error, but you can become a scientific public speaker quickly. For the balance of this chapter, we'll be looking at key principles that virtually all great speakers use and depend upon.

One axiom of public speaking is simple. Don't just make your speech interesting, make it the *most* interesting speech your audience has ever heard. It's not that difficult. All you have to do is talk about the subject that your audience finds more fascinating than any other.

And what is that totally irresistible subject? Well, one of the speakers Dale Carnegie most admired was Russell Conwell. His best-known speech, which he called "Acres of Diamonds," was given nearly six thousand times. You might think that a talk repeated that often would become set in the speaker's mind— that no word or intonation would vary in delivery. But that's not what happened. Russell Conwell knew that no two audiences are alike. He knew that he had to make each new group of listeners feel that he was addressing them and them alone, and that no one had heard this message before. How did Conwell manage to do this from one speaking engagement to the next? "When I visit a town or city," he wrote, "I try to arrive early enough to see the barber, the hotel manager, the principal of the schools, and some of the ministers. Then I go into the shops and just talk with people. I learn their history, and what opportunities they had. When I give my lecture, I know exactly how to deliver each phrase. Even though the message may be the same as in all my previous talks, the actual speech I deliver is now entirely unique."

Successful communication depends upon how well a speaker can make his talk a part of the listeners—and also the listeners a part of the talk. That is why there is no definitive text of the "Acres of Diamonds" speech, despite that it is one of the most popular talks ever given.

Keep this example in mind as you prepare to give a talk. Make certain that you have the specifics of your audience clearly in mind. Make a point of bringing local people and local issues into your talk. Your audiences will be interested because the speech will seem to be about them—about *their* interests, *their* problems, *their* hopes and dreams. Never forget that your listeners are most interested in themselves. By creating a linkage between this interest and whatever your topic might be, you can guarantee the rapt attention of your audience. So axiom number one is, no matter what you're talking about, connect it directly to the self-interest of your listeners.

A second axiom is also focused on appreciating your audience, but in a subtle and irresistible way. There's nothing dishonest about this because you should be totally sincere about it. Simply put, you should express genuine, sincere appreciation for the opportunity to address your listeners.

Audiences are composed of individuals, and they react like

individuals. If you openly criticize them, they will quite naturally resent it. But if you show appreciation for something they've done, you can win their hearts. Regardless of how much or how little you may know about a specific group of listeners, you *do* know that they've asked you to speak. So communicate appreciation for that. Moreover, find a creative way to do it that expresses both your excitement and your sincerity. You see, no matter how naive or unintelligent the individual members of an audience might be, *as a group* they're incredibly perceptive. An insincere statement may fool an individual, but if you're addressing a large group of people, you'll never get away with it. So don't try to fake it. Find a way to feel really grateful for this opportunity, then clearly express that feeling.

An excellent way to start showing appreciation is by immediately identifying yourself with the audience. Break down the distinction between *you* and *them*. As soon as possible, perhaps even with the first words out of your mouth, indicate some direct relationship with the group you're addressing. Whether you know it or not, that relationship does exist. Your job is to find it and use it. When Harold Macmillan, the prime minister of England, addressed the graduating class at DePauw University in Greencastle, Indiana, the connection between the speaker and the audience may not have seemed obvious to his listeners. But Macmillan dealt with that in his first sentence. He mentioned that his mother was an American, born in Indiana, and that her father had been one of DePauw's first graduates. It's a small world, right? By establishing the connection between the school and his own family, Macmillan immediately won friends.

Our next axiom reflects that speaking is not just an audio

medium. Effective speakers know how to use visual stimuli to enhance what they have to say. So don't just reach your readers through their ears. Eye contact is also a hugely important way of connecting. When you speak, it's really your eyes that involve your listeners in your presentation. There's no surer way to break the bond between you and the audience than by failing to look at your listeners.

No matter how many people may be present, every one of them wants to feel that you're focused on him or her alone. Only by looking at your listeners as individuals can you convince them that you're sincerely interested in them, and that you care whether they accept your message. Eye contact also benefits you as a speaker. Your eyes assure you of the attention and concentration of your audience. By looking from one person to another, you can determine how well your message is being received. When you develop the ability to gauge the audience's reactions and adjust your presentation accordingly, you will be a much more effective speaker.

The importance of eye contact is often overlooked, and it's a powerful tool once you learn how to use it. To see how this works, try this exercise. The next time you're watching a movie, notice how much of your attention is directed at the eyes of the actors on the screen—not at their hands, not at their costumes, but at their eyes. Once you become aware of this, you'll see how experienced actors use their eyes to communicate every kind of thought and emotion. This skill takes a long time to learn, but it's one of the defining qualities of good actors, and of great speakers as well.

No one is better at this than Johnny Depp, especially in the *Pirates of the Caribbean* films. As Captain Jack Sparrow,

Johnny Depp may be saying one thing, but his eyes show that his thoughts and feelings are completely the opposite. Johnny Depp learned this technique by studying the great actors of the silent-film era—especially Charlie Chaplin. Obviously, silent-film actors couldn't develop their characters through the spoken word, so they created a whole vocabulary of emotions that were communicated entirely with their eyes. As a speaker, don't overlook the opportunity to make or emphasize a point through the power of a glance. Remember, your listeners have their eyes on you. More specifically, they have *their* eyes on *your* eyes. So take advantage of that.

As you'll recall from chapter 1, memorizing a speech word for word is a bad idea. But bringing some notes to the podium can be useful, and not just because of what's written down. If you watch experienced speakers, you'll notice how they use their notes as a prop to establish a rhythm with the audience—and their eyes are the principal tool for doing this. When making an especially important point, a good speaker will be looking directly at the audience, perhaps even at an individual member of the audience. Then, after the point has been made, the speaker may turn his eyes toward some notes for a moment or two, which gives the audience a moment to absorb what they've just heard. Then, when the speaker looks up again, it's like the beginning of a new talk with a whole new infusion of energy.

Your physical appearance is another important, nonaudio aspect of good speaking. When you're standing in front of people for a substantial time, they have a chance to check you out closely. Every detail of what you wear should be the result of a conscious decision on your part, because at the end of your speech, some people may not know what you said, but virtually all of them will know what kind of shoes you were wearing or whether your tie was crooked. So make sure that every item of your clothing is clean and well tailored. Don't wear jewelry that might glitter or jingle when you move or gesture. Most important, try to dress to match the style and level of your listeners' attire. If you're addressing a NASCAR convention, you might try wearing a cowboy hat, but don't do it when you address the school board. As with eye contact, it's amazing how often this basic tactical principle is ignored, so as you're preparing your speech, spend a moment or two in front of a full-length mirror in the outfit you intend to wear. It's a chance to be proud of how great you look, and it might also be a chance to save yourself some embarrassment.

A final visual aspect of effective speaking is the way you move in front of the audience—or whether you move at all. As always, this should be a conscious choice, and it should start at the moment after you're introduced. You should walk briskly, purposefully, confidently, and calmly to your speaking position. Have a smile on your face or at least a pleasant expression. Even if you're terrified of what you're about to do, try to relax. Initially, don't look at the audience. Look instead at the person who has just introduced you and greet that person with a handshake and a word of thanks. Then pause, arrange your notes if you have any, and finally turn your gaze toward your listeners.

Does all this sound familiar? In a later chapter, we'll have much more to say about how to win over an audience in the first minute. But for now we'll just suggest that you close your eyes and imagine every good speaker you've ever seen when he or she first mounted the stage. The sequence is so well established that you can probably see it with absolute clarity. All you have to do is imitate what you see in your mind's eye. You may not have done it a million times, but you've probably seen it a million times. So just do it on your own.

As you get into your presentation, you may feel confident enough to move away from the lectern or podium. But if you do, you should know where you're going. You shouldn't be just wandering around, nor should you just exchange one fixed position for another. Often, speakers move out from behind the podium, but then stop right beside it and never move again. Like so many other aspects of public speaking, the correct way to move around has actually been well documented and is simple.

Think of your initial position behind the lectern as your home base. Now identify two other positions as alternative bases. As your talk progresses, you're going to be moving among those three locations, and *only* those three locations. Further, your movements should be dictated by the content of your material, not just by your desire to take a stroll. Just as when you consult your notes, moving from one point to another can give your listeners a chance to absorb what you've just said—or it can provide an infusion of energy for a point you're about to make.

As with every other aspect of your speech, the way you move in front of your audience is something you should practice beforehand. Remember, everything about great public speaking only *looks* natural. Nobody was born knowing how to talk, let alone talk in order to captivate others.

With all the excitement you're creating in your talk, you don't want to lose track of time. Many talks can be informative and exciting, but it's rare for people to wish that they went on longer than they did. You don't have to tell people how long your presentation is going to be, but you can rest assured they're wondering about it. So err on the side of caution. When you feel you've got your talk well prepared, try cutting it a bit. No one will mind, and by lowering the word count you may force yourself to say things more directly and powerfully.

When speakers create a checklist of topics, the list becomes a kind of clock in its own right. Telling your listeners how many points you're going to cover can give them a sense that you're well organized and prepared, but if the number is more than three, you're better off keeping that information to yourself. If you've ever been at a presentation where the speaker promised to discuss seven topics, you know why this is true. It's difficult not to start counting on your fingers, trying to figure out how much is still to come. And if you're the speaker, it's hard to keep track of where you are on the shopping list unless you consult your notes, which doesn't support the impression of being well-organized you were trying to create in the first place. In an upcoming chapter you'll learn why three is the magic number when it comes to presentations. Anything beyond that isn't really public speaking. It's higher mathematics.

We've covered a lot of ground in this chapter. Since we've discussed some of the absolute essentials of talking to an audience, you might want to read it again before going on to chapter 3.

But don't delay too long, because chapter 3 will cover one of the most prevalent issues in public speaking. It's commonly called stage fright, but as you'll see, it's not really the stage that we need be frightened of. As a great public speaker once said, "We have nothing to fear but fear itself."

Winston Churchill

Winston Churchill is widely recognized as one of the greatest public speakers in history. Interestingly, Churchill was born with a serious speech impediment. As a young man, he worked tirelessly to overcome the impediment. When listening to Churchill's strong and inspiring speeches, it's hard to imagine that his voice had ever been impaired. Churchill's speeches were especially effective at a time when his country faced its most difficult dilemmas and badly needed courage and inspiration.

One such time was after the Battle of France. Allied forces were surrounded and faced annihilation, and Operation Dynamo was launched to evacuate the troops. In an extraordinary effort, the British army fought off the Luftwaffe, allowing thousands of ships to carry more than three hundred thousand British and French troops to safety—far more than anyone had thought possible.

On June 4, 1940, Winston Churchill gave a speech to the House of Commons in which he had to accomplish a number of objectives simultaneously. First, he had to celebrate the miraculous effort, then he had to tamp down a too optimistic view of what was, in reality, a military disaster, and finally, he had to inspire a country to keep fighting.

*   *   *

During the first four years of the last war the Allies experienced nothing but disaster and disappointment. That was our constant fear: one blow after another, terrible losses, frightful dangers. Everything miscarried. And yet at the end of those four years the morale of the Allies was higher than that of the Germans, who had moved from one aggressive triumph to another, and who stood everywhere triumphant invaders of the lands into which they had broken. During that war we repeatedly asked ourselves the question: "How are we going to win?" And no one was able ever to answer it with much precision, until at the end, quite suddenly, quite unexpectedly, our terrible foe collapsed before us, and we were so glutted with victory that in our folly we threw it away. . . .

However matters may go in France or with the French Government, or other French Governments, we in this Island and in the British Empire will never lose our sense of comradeship with the French people. If we are now called upon to endure what they have been suffering, we shall emulate their courage, and if final victory rewards our toils they shall share the gains, aye, and freedom shall be restored to all. We abate nothing of our just demands; not one jot or tittle do we recede. Czechs, Poles, Norwegians, Dutch, Belgians, have joined their causes to our own. All these shall be restored.

What General Weygand called the Battle of France is over. I expect that the Battle of Britain is about to begin. Upon this battle depends the survival of Christian civilization. Upon it depends our own British life, and the long continuity of our institutions and our Empire. The whole fury and might of the enemy must very soon be turned on us.

Hitler knows that he will have to break us in this Island or lose the war. If we can stand up to him, all Europe may be free and the life of the world may move forward into broad, sunlit uplands. But if we fail, then the whole world, including the United States, including all that we have known and cared for, will sink into the abyss of a new Dark Age made more sinister, and perhaps more protracted, by the lights of perverted science.

Let us therefore brace ourselves to our duties, and so bear ourselves that if the British Empire and its Commonwealth last for a thousand years, men will still say, "This was their finest hour."

When a sermon at length comes to an end, people rise and praise God, and they feel the same way after many other speeches.

—John Andrew Holmes

A speech is poetry: cadence, rhythm, imagery, sweep! A speech reminds us that words, like children, have the power to make dance the dullest beanbag of a heart.

—Peggy Noonan

The nature of oratory is such that there has always been a tendency among politicians and clergymen to oversimplify complex matters. From a pulpit or a platform even the most conscientious of speakers finds it very difficult to tell the whole truth.

—Aldous Huxley

CHAPTER 3

Overcoming Stage Fright:
"Nothing to Fear but Fear Itself"

This is an important chapter! To begin, here are some thoughts on fear that the great Earl Nightingale shared in one of his presentations.

Two young boys were raised by an alcoholic father. As they grew older, they moved away from that broken home, each going his own way in the world. Several years later, they happened to be interviewed separately by a psychologist who was analyzing the effects of drunkenness on children in broken homes. His research revealed that the two men were strikingly different from each other. One was a clean-living teetotaler; the other, a hopeless drunk like his father. The psychologist asked each of them why he developed the way he did, and each gave an identical answer, "What else would you expect when you have a father like mine?"

Dr. Hans Selye, an internationally renowned Canadian physician, was known as the "father of fear." A medical pioneer, he devoted the majority of his years to the exploration of fear's biological foundations. And he related the story of the two sons of the drunken father in an article for New Realities.

The story demonstrates a cardinal rule implicit in fear, stress, health, and human behavior in general: "It is not what happens to you

*in life that makes the difference. It is how you react to each circum-
stance you encounter that determines the result. Every human being in
the same situation has the possibilities of choosing how he will react,
which might be either positively or negatively."*

*Thus, fear is not necessarily caused by stressor agents; rather, it is
caused by the way stressor agents are perceived, interpreted, or ap-
praised in each individual case. Outside events and people upset some
more than others, because they are looked upon and dealt with in entirely different ways. The stressors may even be the same in each case,
yet the reaction will almost always be different in different people.*

Fear of speaking in public is often cited as people's biggest fear
of all. Getting up in front of an audience makes many people
uncomfortable. But as you're about to learn, anxiety about
public speaking can quickly be brought under control with just
a little effort and information. That's why the title of chapter
3 says "Nothing to Fear but Fear Itself." If there's one topic
where that famous precept is right on the money, this is it.

When people say they're afraid of speaking in public, what
is it that they're really afraid of? Unless you're addressing a
hostile audience in some dangerous region of the world, you
probably don't have to worry about physical violence. Even if
you suddenly draw a complete blank when you get behind the
podium, it's unlikely the audience will throw things or laugh
out loud at you. On the contrary, everyone knows that making
presentations is a challenge, so your audience would probably
be sympathetic. So let's look carefully at what people are really
afraid of, then see how to deal with that fear.

The fear of self. Just plain self-consciousness, a feeling that
expresses itself in the mental question "What in blazes am

I doing this for? How in the world did I get myself into this situation?"

Reflections from the past. The remembrance, even subliminally, of old classroom failures; being laughed at or ridiculed.

Overconcern about what others think. The questioning of our authority to be talking before such a group.

Poor preparation. The panicky feeling that the speech needs work or complete overhauling or throwing away.

Lack of courage to try new things. The fear of doing the unusual.

Lack of encouragement from others. I know it always helps me tremendously to hear a comment such as "The group is looking forward to hearing what you have to say."

What should you do about these problems?

- Recognize that others have the same fears.

- Try to analyze what and why you fear.

- Find a compulsion to speak; realize that you have important things to say and that you want to say them.

- Be prepared.

- Take a course.

- Actually doing it; there's nothing like it.

- Talk only on subjects you know well, subjects you're an expert on and feel comfortable with.

You see, it's not totally blowing it that we fear. *It's being any-thing less than perfect.* Nervous public speakers aren't afraid of striking out. They're afraid of not hitting a grand-slam home run. They're afraid, for example, that they'll be recognized as being afraid—and that only makes the fear worse. For some reason, perfectionism seems to be built into the concept of public speaking, yet perfectionism is just the opposite of what a good speaker should be feeling. This is true not only emotion-ally, but physically as well.

You've probably heard of the so-called fight-or-flight re-sponse. It's the primal yes-or-no question that your brain asks when you're faced with a stress-inducing situation. It's the hardwired prehistoric choice that still exists in our minds, even in the twenty-first century. Are we going to confront this threat like a good caveman or cavewoman? Or are we going to run to the back of the cave and hide from it? Never mind that what we're confronting is not a mammoth, but the weekly meeting of the PTA. At the deepest level, the human brain doesn't make those kinds of distinctions. When you're feeling stressed by an unfamiliar circumstance, your brain thinks ev-erything is on the line.

The fight-or-flight response leads to some well-documented physical reactions, and a couple of them are unfortunate in pub-lic speaking. It doesn't really matter that the pupils of your eyes dilate, or that your digestive system begins to shut down. But the fight-or-flight response also causes a powerful inhibition of the vocal cords. At the neurobiological level, the ability to talk is blocked. Your capability to speak is actually paralyzed. As if that weren't enough, your facial muscles can also freeze up. So you're not able to say anything, and you're not even able to grin and bear it. The fight-or-flight response has turned you into a stone statue. This is exactly what you were afraid of, right? And that's exactly why it happened: because you were afraid!

Many highly accomplished public speakers continue to experience stage fright, regardless of how many talks they've given. They accept that as a fact of life. They don't have to completely erase the fear in order to bring it under control. They're pragmatists rather than perfectionists. Stage fright may come and go, but it does not usually permanently vanish. The secret to success is putting fright into the proper perspective and channeling it in a positive way.

Dale Carnegie was not a physician or a neurologist, but he was definitely a pioneer in dealing effectively with public-speaking anxiety. He liked to tell the story of an executive who joined his public-speaking course in Philadelphia. This man had always led an active life. He owned a manufacturing company and was a leader in church work and civic activities. But before the first class with Dale Carnegie, he confessed, "I've been asked many times to speak before various gatherings, but I have never been able to accept any of those invitations. If I even think about standing up at the front of a room, my mind just goes blank. And now I've been invited to join the board of trustees at my college alma mater. It's a great honor, but I'll have to preside at meetings and I'll definitely have to do some talking. Do you think I can learn to handle something like that at this point in my life?"

Dale Carnegie's reply, as he later described it, was straightforward: "It's not a question of what I think. I *know* you can do this, and I know you will if you just pay attention and practice what you learn."

The executive wanted to believe what he'd just heard, but it seemed too rosy, too optimistic. "You're just trying to be kind," he said. "You're trying to encourage me."

At the end of the course, he and Dale Carnegie lost touch for several years. But when they finally met again, Carnegie asked if he had been too optimistic in their previous conversation. So the executive took a notebook from his pocket and revealed a list of upcoming talks and meetings. Not only had he given many public presentations of various kinds, but he was developing a whole new career as a speaker. "And this was the man," Dale Carnegie wrote, "who had solemnly asked me if I thought he would ever be able to talk in public!"

Most people make rapid progress once they approach public speaking in an organized way, and this is especially true when it comes to overcoming fear. The Dale Carnegie organization has worked with literally thousands of people in this area and is continually updating its techniques. We've mentioned just one client, but there are many more. For instance, there was a New York City physician—we can call him Dr. Curtis—who liked to take vacations in Florida near the spring-training camp of the Los Angeles Dodgers. He often went to see them practice, and over time he became friendly with the players and the team manager. One year he was invited to attend a banquet given at the end of spring training.

Toward the end of the dinner, as coffee was served, several guests were invited to "say a few words." As much as he had enjoyed himself that evening, this made Dr. Curtis extremely uneasy—and suddenly, like an explosion, his worst fear came true. He heard the team manager say, "We happen to have a man with us tonight who is both a real baseball fan and a very talented physician. I'd appreciate it if Dr. Curtis would speak for a moment on the health concerns of major league ballplayers."

The doctor could hardly believe this was happening. He had had no idea that he would be asked to speak. Was he prepared? Well, in one sense he had the best preparation in the world. He had been practicing medicine for thirty years. He could have talked all night to the man seated on his right about any aspect of physical health. But to get up and say the same things to even a small audience—that was another matter. For that, he was totally *un*prepared. His heart raced. His palms sweated. His throat was dry. He had never made a public speech in his life, and whatever he knew about this subject flew out the window.

What was he going to do? The audience was applauding. Everyone was looking at him. He hesitated, but that only heightened the applause and increased the demand. There were cries of "Dr. Curtis! Speech! Speech!"

The physician was in misery. He knew that if he stood up, he would be unable to utter half a dozen sentences. So he rose and, without saying a word, turned his back on his friends and walked silently out of the room. It couldn't possibly have been worse.

Dr. Curtis didn't want to face that situation ever again. As soon as he got back to New York, he enrolled in Dale Carnegie's public-speaking course, and he never missed a single class. As a result, he progressed at a rate that surpassed anything he could have expected. After the first few classes his nervousness subsided, and over the coming weeks his confidence soared. In two months, he had become the star speaker of the class. Not only that, but he was soon accepting invitations to speak elsewhere. In less than a year, it seemed impossible that he would ever have walked out of a banquet because he was afraid to get up and talk.

Self-confidence and courage while talking to a group are nowhere near as hard as people imagine. It's not a gift bestowed on only a few lucky individuals. You learned to talk, which is probably the greatest intellectual accomplishment of anyone's life. Having done this, you can also learn to talk in public—no matter how frightening that prospect now seems. Anyone can develop that ability if there's real desire to do so.

Stage fright isn't really an accurate term for the anxiety that often accompanies a speaking engagement. Actually, most of the fear occurs *before* you step onstage. Once people are up there, it usually goes away for most of them. Being nervous even has some positive side effects. It makes your reflexes sharper and heightens your energy. When you are nervous about speaking, you may be conscious of your posture and breathing. Many people actually look healthier and more attractive on the outside precisely because of their inner distress.

Even experienced speakers have a sense of responsibility in giving a talk. This sense of responsibility can range from barely suppressed panic to outward exhilaration. Two thousand years ago, the Roman orator Cicero said that all public speaking of real merit was characterized by nervousness, so a good speaker is always keyed up before an event, like a Thoroughbred straining at the bit.

Even Abraham Lincoln felt shy in the few opening moments of a talk. As his law partner William Herndon described it, "Lincoln was always very awkward at first, and it seemed a real labor to adjust himself to his surroundings. I have often seen and sympathized with Mr. Lincoln during those moments. When he began speaking, his voice was shrill, piping, and unpleasant. His manner, his attitude, his oddity of pose—everything seemed to be against him. But this only lasted for a short time. In a few moments he always gained composure and warmth and earnestness, and then his real speech began."

Your experience may be similar to Lincoln's, in which case you'll be in good company. But to master the art of public speaking as quickly as possible, four things are absolutely essential.

First, start with a strong and persistent desire to speak and connect with the audience. This is more important than you may realize. If an experienced public speaker could look into your heart right now, he or she could foretell almost with certainty the success you will have—based simply on how much you want it. If you go after this subject with persistence and energy, nothing can deter you.

So arouse your enthusiasm for this opportunity. Focus on the benefits. Think of what the ability to talk more convincingly will mean to you, both personally and in dollars and cents. Think of what it can mean to you socially—of the friends it will bring you, of the influence it will confer on you, of the leadership it will impart to you. Being able to express yourself well in public will make you a leader more quickly than any other activity you could imagine.

This is true now, and it has always been true. A hundred years ago, Andrew Carnegie was the wealthiest and most influential businessman in America. After his death in 1919, among his papers was found a plan for his life drawn up when he was thirty-three years old. He felt that in two more years he would be able to retire. Then he hoped to attend Oxford University for a classical education, including, as he put it, "special attention to speaking in public." Although Carnegie did not retire as he planned, he remained totally in awe of the ability to speak well. He was much more impressed by this talent than by the ability to make money, which may have been because he himself was one of the richest men in the world.

In every field, a certain percentage of people give up before they fulfill their potential and reach their goals. Their desire to succeed is simply not equal to the effort that success demands. As you go through this book, and especially this section on overcoming fear, you should keep thinking of what success will mean to you until your desire is white-hot. Start this learning experience with an enthusiasm that will carry you through to the end. Do everything to reinforce that enthusiasm. Tell your friends that you have decided to improve your speaking skills. Set aside a specific time each day for reading the book and practicing what you learn. Make it as easy as possible to move forward. Make it as difficult as possible to retreat.

As Dale Carnegie said, few things compare to standing before an audience and transferring what is in your mind to theirs. A kind of magic is in it. "Two minutes before I begin," one speaker confessed, "I would rather be shot than go ahead. But two minutes before I finish, I would rather be shot than stop."

If overwhelming desire is the first step to conquering fear, thorough knowledge is the second. Before you talk, you must know what you are going to talk about thoroughly. Unless you know exactly what you are going to say, you can't feel comfortable when you face your audience. If you're that uncomfortable, you *ought* to be self-conscious, you *ought* to feel repentant, and you *ought* to be ashamed of your negligence.

Have a message, then think of yourself as a messenger instructed to deliver it. People pay little attention to a messenger. It is the message that they want. So keep your mind on it. Keep your heart in it. Know it like the back of your hand. Believe it, and speak as if you were determined to say it. Do that, and you will soon be master of the audience and master of yourself.

"When I was elected to the New York State Legislature," Theodore Roosevelt wrote in his autobiography, "I found myself the youngest man there. I had difficulty in teaching myself to speak. I profited from some good advice, which ran: 'Don't speak until you are sure you have something to say and you know just what it is. Then say it. And then sit down.'"

Here's some more advice that might have benefited Roosevelt, and that will certainly benefit you: if you can find some prop to use in front of your audience, it will help defuse your anxiety. Show them something, write a word on a blackboard, point out a spot on a map, move a table, open a window—any physical action with a purpose behind it will help you to feel more at home.

So desire comes first, then knowledge—and confidence is next. William James, the great American psychologist, wrote, "Action seems to follow feeling, but really action and feeling go together. By regulating our actions, which are under our direct control, we can regulate our feelings, which are not."

To feel brave, apply William James's advice and act as if you were brave. To develop courage when you are facing an audience, act as if you already had it. Of course, unless you are prepared, all the acting in the world won't help. But once you know what you are going to talk about, step out briskly and take a deep breath. In fact, breathe deeply for thirty seconds or so before you ever face your audience. Then draw yourself up to your full height and look your audience straight in the eyes—and begin to talk as confidently as if every one of them owed you money. Imagine that they do owe you money. Pretend that they are there to beg you for an extension of credit!

The next point is the most important. Even if you forget everything you have read so far, remember this: the first way, the last way, the never-failing way to develop self-confidence in speaking is . . . to speak. The whole matter finally comes down to but one essential: practice, practice, practice. What public speaking requires is not really courage, but *coolheadedness*. This can only come through experience. It takes continual effort and repeated exercise of willpower.

So keep at it. Fear comes from lack of confidence. Lack of confidence comes from lack of practice. Once you have sufficient practice, your fear will vanish. That's the good news—but it's not the only news. You should also be aware that anxiety about speaking is ongoing. It will need to be managed throughout your speaking career. Even experienced public speakers can quite unexpectedly get nervous about making a presentation. How this can take place is somewhat mysterious, but there's nothing mysterious about how to prevent it.

Becoming a high impact public speaker is never really complete. It's a dynamic experience in which new thoughts and feelings are always appearing. Strangely enough, old feelings can also *re*appear, including stage fright. For the balance of this chapter, we'll look at how and why this happens, and we'll see how you can manage anxiety even if you can't entirely eliminate it.

A recurrence of stage fright can begin innocently. From your vantage point behind the podium, you may notice someone in the front row with a bored expression. You wonder whether your energy level is where it needs to be. Then you see someone whispering something to her neighbor, and you worry that your hair is out of place or your tie is crooked. Or worse yet, maybe you're thinking how completely wrongheaded your ideas are. Pretty soon your palms are sweating, although you thought you'd conquered that long ago. And you're thinking that maybe you're not cut out for this after all.

Sooner or later in your speaking career, something like this will probably happen to you. It happens to almost every speaker, from the beginner to the most seasoned professional. It's how we generate negative thoughts during a presentation, almost as if we want to defeat ourselves.

It all begins with a loss of focus. Some minor distraction occurs, and we become less and less able to concentrate. The result can be nervousness, memory lapse, sudden fear, and general discomfort. Yet the whole problem can often be avoided by keeping a few basic ideas in mind before we stand up to speak. No matter how new or how experienced you may be, run through this mental checklist a few minutes before going onstage. A few moments of prevention are worth many hours of cure.

Start by reminding yourself that you have prepared to the best of your ability. As we discussed in chapter 1, you have done your research and you have done your rehearsals. You may wonder whether you could have done more, but that kind of second-guessing is not appropriate at this moment. Instead, you are going on "automatic pilot." You're going to let your diligent preparation do its work. Tell yourself that the hard part is over. Now you can just trust your preparation to do the work for you. No more effort or worry is required. Everything you need is already here for you.

Next, make yourself a promise to relinquish judgment of your talk during the time it's going on. Self-judgment during a performance is also self-destruction. It takes you out of the present and into the past or future, and it destroys the natural flow of your speech. So rather than judge your talk, simply observe it without any inner commentary but with full inner motivation. When you are about to make a major point, for example, *intend* to do it and then feel it as you *are* doing it. At that moment, you are translating intention into action.

Third, remind yourself not to let the reaction of anyone in the audience influence your performance. Don't let anything you see or hear cause you to second-guess yourself. If you have done a sufficient amount of rehearsing, you may feel that you know how listeners will react to your message. But rehearsal is not a perfect system. The responses of your friends and family can only partly predict what a totally new audience will do. If you start wondering about the guy in the first row, you'll soon be wondering about the other guy in the fourth row, and the upshot will be a major erosion of confidence. Trying to imagine what someone in the audience is thinking is useless and distracting. It's also a big waste of energy. For the time that you're speaking, you need only to please yourself.

In other words, keep your mind onstage, not in the audience. Be in the giving mode, not the receiving one. Be in the moment, and be in the speech. You can't be the speaker and the listener at the same time, so leave the response to the audience. Your task is to communicate what you have thought and felt and practiced. That's all, and that's enough.

Now, just as your talk is about to begin, think about one aspect of your performance that is your top priority. What is the single thing that you most need to remember? Don't think about this while you're talking. Think about it *beforehand*. You may, for instance, want to emphasize good posture. So you remind yourself to stand up straight. Or you can recall the importance of speaking clearly and varying the cadence of your sentences. Although you might like to emphasize dozens of elements, choosing more than one will only diminish the benefits of this exercise. So choose one aspect, and choose it carefully.

But let's allow ourselves another thought, uncomfortable as it may seem. Suppose, just suppose, your whole speech goes to hell in the proverbial handbasket. It has happened to everyone, even the greatest speakers, and it may also happen to you. If and when it does, there's only one question you need to ask yourself: *so what?*

Are you familiar with the old fable about the devil's sale? It's interesting. And like most old fables, it has a moral that's worth thinking about. The story goes that the devil was having a sale of his wares. There on display were the rapier of jealousy, the dagger of fear, and the strangling noose of hatred, each with its own high price. But standing alone on a purple pedestal, gleaming in the light, was a worn and battered wedge. This was the devil's most prized possession. For with it alone, he could stay in business, and this was not for sale. It was the wedge of discouragement.

The devil prizes the wedge of discouragement above all else because of its enfeebling, demoralizing effect. Hatred, fear, or jealousy may lead an immature person to act unwisely, to fight or run or grab, but at least he acts. Discouragement, on the other hand, is more harmful than anything else. It causes you to sit down, pity yourself, and *do nothing*.

This doesn't have to happen, but unfortunately it all too frequently does. Not until we realize that discouragement is often a form of self-pity do we begin to take stock of ourselves and our predicament and decide to act, to do something that will take us out of an unpleasant situation. The answer to discouragement, to self-pity, then, is intelligent action.

The late W. Clement Stone, the billionaire founder of Combined Insurance Company, formed the habit in the early days of his career of saying "Excellent!" whenever anything happened, good or bad. Most of the time, of course, it was something good. But even when he learned of a near calamity, a deadly serious situation that would have sent a lesser man scurrying for cover, he smiled and said, "Excellent!" Then as his associates shook their heads in resigned disbelief, he'd tear headlong into the problem and find what was good in it. Invariably, some elements in the situation could be turned to advantage. He would find them and, more important, act on them.

Everyone has days or even successions of days when nothing seems to go right. Yet if we understand that something good can usually be grounded in almost any situation, we'll go quietly, efficiently to work on the most important part of the problem, the one that can be turned to advantage. Self-pity or inactivity cannot possibly help the situation. The only rational course to follow is to reevaluate and move forward.

Some of the most successful speakers have at some time been forced to analyze their methods and use of time. Things don't always go well. It happens to everybody. A dry spell is no fun for anyone, but it's often only the extreme situation that gets us to look at ourselves: to find out that what we're doing, why we're doing it, and what needs to change to get the best possible result. As Emerson said, "When a man is pushed, tormented, defeated . . . he has a chance to learn something." And Emerson was a noted public speaker.

Discouragement often comes on the heels of a crisis. It's been said that crises are thoroughfares; we can go either way, up or down. We go up out of a crisis by doing something constructive; we go down by wallowing around in our problems and feeling sorry for ourselves. Discouragement, which comes to all of us sooner or later, is a test of nature. Those who refuse to yield to it pass in time through discouragement to the smooth and sunlit seas beyond. What once seemed to be a storm with such voracity that it blotted out the whole world is soon forgotten.

Whenever you face discouragement, try to keep in mind three vitally important points. First, discouragement is often a form of self-pity, an expensive emotion we can get along well without. The most effective antidote for self-pity is intelligent action. Next, within any discouraging situation almost always lurks an opportunity for growth, maturity, and future success. There's something good about it. And, finally, discouragement should be kept in proper perspective. What may at the moment seem like the end of the world won't seem so important in ten days or won't be important in ten months. Take the long-range view and you can't be defeated by momentary setbacks.

The Chinese have a saying: if you live with a disaster for three years, it will turn into a blessing. In other words, failure is delay. Not defeat. It is a temporary detour, not a dead end. Failure is something we can avoid only by saying nothing, doing nothing, and being nothing.

It should motivate you more toward your own goals to know that some of the most famous and well-known people in modern times had to overcome obstacles as difficult as anyone's before they finally reached the top. It takes persistence and total commitment to your goals, but it's possible.

Thomas Edison's father called him a "dunce." Edison's headmaster in school told him he would never make a success of anything.

Henry Ford barely made it through high school.

The machines of the world's greatest inventor, Leonardo da Vinci, were never built, and many wouldn't have worked anyway.

Edwin Land, the inventor of the Polaroid Land camera, failed absolutely at developing instant movies. He described his attempts as trying to use an impossible chemistry and a nonexistent technology to make an unmanufacturable product for which there was no discernible demand. These hurdles, in his opinion, created the optimum working conditions for the creative mind.

Joe Paterno, head coach of the Penn State University football team well into his eighties, was asked by the media how he felt when his team lost a game. He rapidly replied that losing was probably good for the team, since that was how the players learned what they were doing wrong.

Setbacks and failures mean little or nothing in themselves. The whole meaning of any setback—or any success, for that matter—is in how we take it and what we make of it.

We often look at high achievers and assume they had a string of lucky breaks or made it without much effort. Usually the opposite is true, and the so-called superstar or "overnight success" had an incredibly rough time before he or she attained any lasting success.

You may not know the background of a certain laundry worker who earned $60 a week at his job but had the burning desire to be a writer. His wife worked nights, and he spent nights and weekends typing manuscripts to send to publishers and agents. Each one was rejected with a form letter that gave him no assurance that his manuscript had even been read.

But finally, a warm, more personal rejection letter came in the mail to the laundry worker, stating that, although his work was not good enough at this point to warrant publishing, he had promise as a writer and should keep writing.

He forwarded two more manuscripts to the same friendly-yet-rejecting publisher over the next eighteen months, and as before, he struck out with both of them. Finances got so tight for the young couple that they had to disconnect their telephone to pay for medicine for their baby.

Feeling totally discouraged, he threw his latest manuscript into the garbage. His wife, totally committed to his life goals and believing in his talent, took the manuscript out of the trash and sent it to Doubleday, the publisher who had sent the friendly rejections. The book, titled *Carrie*, sold more than 5 million copies and, as a movie, became one of the top-grossing films in 1976. The laundry worker, of course, was Stephen King.

Think back to a time in your life you have found difficult. Try to see what you gained as a result of what you learned, what strength you found even in the most trying time—or what strength you find now in your having overcome it. Perhaps you may never have been aware of what you gained until you think about it now. The Chinese have a saying: "Eat bitter to taste sweet." It means that by living through painful experiences, we can become stronger people. The transformation depends on our ability to discover something beyond the pain.

Finally and most important, make yourself ready to *enjoy* the presentation you're about to give. This is the time when you can finally share with your listeners what you have worked so hard to achieve. This is a time of joy, not a time for correcting real or imagined errors. There will be time for that later. Right now, let the thoughts and emotions of your speech take over. Don't allow minor details to obscure your feelings. Let your excitement for the opportunity be present. Let your passion as a speaker show through—because the only thing you have to fear *really is* fear itself.

Always be shorter than anybody dared to hope.

—Lord Reading

Oratory is the power to talk people out of their sober and natural opinions.

—Joseph Chatfield

The eloquent man is he who is no beautiful speaker, but who is inwardly and desperately drunk with a certain belief.

—Ralph Waldo Emerson

CHAPTER 4

Using Humor Effectively

Oscar Wilde said, "It is a curious fact that the worst work is always done with the best intentions, and that people are never so trivial as when they take themselves very seriously."

Of course, that doesn't mean we should never be serious. When someone is ill or hurt, the situation can get serious in a hurry. But taking yourself seriously is something entirely different.

A good rule of thumb with regard to a public speaker is this: be slightly suspicious of anyone who takes himself too seriously. There's usually something fishy there, something dishonest or unnatural. That kind of seriousness is being "grown-up" in the worst sense of the term. For children, on the other hand, so much of life is a game. They will do their best at whatever work is given them, but they never seem to lose their ebullient sense of humor; a sparkle of humor is always in their eyes. We love this in kids, and we love it in speakers as well.

Dictators are famous for their lack of humor. The mark of a cruel person is that he doesn't seem able to see anything funny in the world. Mark Twain's sense of humor was the key to his greatness, and he was undoubtedly the most popular speaker of his time. No matter how serious the subject, he could find its humor and bring it out. So many great speakers have the ability to see what's funny in a so-called serious situation. They can poke fun at themselves. Some believe that a sense of humor is the only thing that has kept the human race from totally extinguishing itself.

People who are emotionally healthy, with a sense of proportion, are cheerful. They tend to look upon the bright side of things and have humor in their daily lives. They're not fools—they know what's going on in the world and that a lot of it is not funny—but they don't permit that dark side to dominate their lives. As the novelist Samuel Butler said, "A sense of humor keen enough to show a man his own absurdities as well as those of other people will keep a man from the commission of all sins, or nearly all, save those that are worth committing."

It took a sense of humor to write that, and only people with a blank space where their sense of humor should be will find it offensive. Something about laughter is so healthy, especially when it's directed at ourselves.

For all of us, at times all the laughter seems to be gone, but we should not permit these periods to last too long. When we've lost our sense of humor, there isn't much left. We become ridiculous. We must then go to war against the whole world, and that's a war we can't win.

So humor can undoubtedly be a powerful resource for public speaking. But it's not just a laughing matter. It must be used carefully, and at times it shouldn't be used at all. If you can convey your message in an amusing and entertaining manner, that's great. But if humor is used awkwardly or distastefully, you can seriously damage your cause.

It's not always easy to know when humor is appropriate and

when it isn't because on this subject everyone seems to consider himself an expert. It's rare to hear someone say, "I just don't have a good sense of humor." And it's difficult to prove that person wrong because humor is totally subjective. If you say that you can beat the Wimbledon champion in a tennis match, an objective way exists to prove whether that's true. The proof will appear on the scoreboard. But if you say that there's nothing funny about *Seinfeld*, it's completely a matter of opinion. Even if everyone else in the room is laughing at the show, you can shrug your shoulders and say they're wrong. They just don't have good taste, and you do.

In public speaking, however, it doesn't really matter whether *you* think something is funny. What matters is what the audience thinks. So while in theory every speech can benefit from a humorous element, in practice this depends on several variables—and what's the most important variable? Let's answer that question with more questions: Are you funny or aren't you? Can you use humor effectively or not?

It's not easy to find simple answers to these questions. You've probably met people who could not tell a joke if their life depended on it. Yet those people might actually be funny individuals precisely because they're so inept at being funny. If any general statement can be made about humor in public speaking, it might be this: all people can use humor effectively, once they find the type of humor that fits their personality and speaking style. It all comes back to that axiom we mentioned at the start of the book: *know thyself.* So as you read the ideas and concepts of this chapter, ask yourself whether you would feel comfortable building them into your live presentations. Humor is too serious to be taken lightly, but it's also an extremely potent attribute to have in your public-speaking arsenal. So let's get started. Did you hear the one about the duck who complained to the electric company? He was angry about his bill.

Just kidding! But did you laugh? If not, it may be because the joke wasn't funny. But it might also be because you weren't expecting to read a joke in a book on public speaking. This leads to an important insight about the nature of humor. When you go to the movies to see a comedy, you may have noticed an interesting phenomenon: the audience usually starts laughing before anything funny has happened. The beginning of the movie can be totally without humorous content, but people still laugh. Why? Well, they bought tickets to a comedy, and the purpose of comedy is to evoke laughter, so they laugh whether or not anything funny is actually happening.

By understanding what this means, you can gain some useful insights about humor. You'll see why bringing humor into a speech is more than just a way to add entertainment value. Instead, it's fulfilling a basic need of the audience's. People don't just want to laugh, they *need* to laugh. If you can help them do that, it's just as if you've given food to a hungry person. You've not only made their lives easier, you've actually helped them survive. And as a result, they'll be receptive to your message.

It's often been pointed out that human beings are the only animals that laugh. But what do we actually laugh at? Is it possible to make a general statement about what people think is funny? Or, let's start small. Can you even say what *you yourself* think is funny in any kind of a general way?

So the next time you hear people in an audience laugh, ask yourself, "What's so funny?" As we've mentioned, quite often the answer is "Nothing." The laughter isn't because anything hilarious is happening on the screen at the theater. It's happening because the audience *needs to laugh.* In a similar way, if you see a hundred people eating dinner in a restaurant, it may be because the food is great, but even if it isn't so great, they will still continue eating because they *need* to eat. At dinnertime or lunchtime most people are hardwired to eat, so they do. What's more, you can get them to eat in your restaurant even if you're not the greatest chef in the world. You just have to connect with their built-in need to eat and fulfill that need to a serviceable level.

That's why a talent for being funny is not essential for using humor effectively in a presentation. What *is* essential is the *desire* to be funny, and the ability to communicate that desire to your listeners. If you can show your audience that you at least want them to laugh, they're certain to go along with you because, remember, laughter is something they need. The only way you can fail with humor is when people aren't sure what you want them to do. If they know they've bought a ticket to a comedy, they'll act the way they're supposed to act at a comedy. But if they're not sure what kind of a show they're seeing, they won't be in their "funny gear." And if they're not in their funny gear, they're not going to laugh because they're not sure that's what they're supposed to do.

When an audience is in funny gear, they'll take your humor and words in a playful way and enjoy them. But if they're in "serious gear," nothing will make them laugh. Either they won't understand what they're supposed to do, or they'll resent that they're now being asked to laugh by somebody that they don't think is funny.

Humor can't be forced, nor should it be reached for. It comes naturally to those with the ability, or at least it seems to. If you have it, congratulations. Use it wisely. If you don't have it, use it sparingly and make certain something's really funny before you use it at all. Don't dabble in one of the most difficult professions in the world—that of a stand-up comedian.

Before you include a joke in your speech, ask yourself, "Why am I telling it?" Jokes aren't *necessary* to the opening of a speech. Neither are funny comments, unless they have a clever tie-in of some sort that the audience will genuinely appreciate and enjoy.

So many ineffective speakers say, following the introduction, "That reminds me of a story . . . ," then tell a story that hasn't the faintest relevance to anything said in the introduction. It didn't remind him. He just wanted to tell a joke, and all those in the audience know it and begin to move their feet and cough and look around for the exit.

Here's a good rule to follow. If there is any doubt in your mind whatsoever, if there is the faintest feeling of uneasiness about a story, don't tell it. That feeling of uneasiness is your more intelligent subconscious trying to tell you to forget it. Save it for the locker room at the club if you must tell it.

If you want a foolproof system, use the enormously successful technique used by everyone from Jack Benny to Steve Martin to Conan O'Brien: make yourself the joke. Jack Benny once produced the most prolonged, helpless laughter in the history of show business. It happened on his old radio program when he was approached by a robber who said, "Your money or your life." What followed was simply silence, the deadly, convulsively funny silence that only Jack Benny could manage. The silence lasted only a few seconds before the laughter began, then mounted and mounted and continued for a record-breaking fifteen minutes or so. Finally, when it did subside, the robber repeated, "I said your money or your life." And Jack Benny replied, "I'm thinking. I'm thinking."

Again the laughter took hold, and the program nearly ran out of time before it could even attempt to finish. A simple silence did it as Jack tried desperately to decide which was more important to him, his money or his life. He was always the loser in his elaborate plans, as is the coyote in his attempts to trap the roadrunner. People love when we're foiled by our own weaknesses.

If humor is your strength, then you don't need any advice or help from me. If it isn't, use it sparingly and in good taste. It's wonderful when it's right. It's the opposite of wonderful when it isn't.

To help with all this, experienced speakers sometimes use a simple test. Before they go out to face the audience, they ask the host of the event to put a little joke into the introduction. From the audience response, the speaker can tell how receptive they'll be to a humorous approach. If the audience isn't ready and expecting to laugh, trying to use humor could backfire. You must be able to read your audience accurately. It's better to not go for a laugh than try for one and come up empty.

Once listeners are primed for humor, a basic shift occurs in the way they see the world. Pleasant things are still seen in a positive light, but even some usually disagreeable things provoke a laugh. This leads to a key point about humor. Painful things told playfully are a huge resource of laughs, but it's got to be done carefully. For example, it's okay to make fun of other people, but this can never seem mean-spirited. The simple rule for handling this is, don't try to laugh about traits that people can't control or change. You can make a joke about someone who doesn't know how to park a car, but not about someone who got hit by a car.

The single exception to this is if the person hit by the car was *you*. You are always fair game for your own humor. So in breaking the ice and becoming a welcome speaker, there is no better way than to make yourself the butt of the joke. Self-effacing humor is always safe in that you appear human to your audience and you do not risk offending them in any way. The more you make fun of yourself, the more you're allowed to make fun of other things, including other people. So an excellent rule of thumb to follow is, get at least one laugh at your own expense before you try to get a laugh at anything else. Then weave self-deprecating humor into any other humorous material in your speech.

These are general rules, and the specific type of humor you should use depends on your speaking style. Are you more comfortable with quiet, subtle wit, or are you more likely to go after big laughs? Or, if you're like many people, maybe you're not sure right now what kind of humor best fits your personal style. So let's take a quick look at some different types of humor, and as you'll see, there are a lot of them. Some of them may seem very funny to you, while others may strike you as exactly the opposite. As you read this survey, see which categories of humor seem like the best fit with your personality. Also, feel free to laugh, because your own laughter is probably the best guide to the right kind of humor for you.

One of the most powerful tools of humorous public speaking is the anecdote. To define exactly what an anecdote is, we can contrast it with its close relative, the joke. A joke is a brief narrative with a humorous climactic twist. An anecdote is also a narrative, but it is usually not as brief as a joke. Also, the humorous content of an anecdote is not generally saved until the end. An anecdote can be funny all the way through, or it can also be not funny, if the speaker chooses. But the power of a joke depends on our not acknowledging any humorous content until the punch line. For many people, the very idea of a duck telephoning the electric company might seem funny, but we put that humor aside to finally let it go in the closing line.

The greater flexibility of the anecdote as opposed to the joke is what makes the anecdote such a valuable device. At the end of his life, financial pressures forced Mark Twain to embark on extended lecture tours all over the world. In these lectures he told the same anecdotes over and over—and, amazingly, the result was always the same. His audiences went crazy with laughter. People who heard Twain's lectures reported that some of his listeners actually seemed to be in pain because they were laughing so hard. To some extent, Twain's anecdotes had this effect simply because the content of the stories was funny. But more important, he was able to shorten or lengthen or otherwise adjust the anecdotes based on his understanding of the audience. This isn't really possible with a joke, in which the times between beginning, middle, and end are predetermined. With this in mind, effective public speakers always have a stockpile of humorous anecdotes, informative stories, and inspirational narratives. Moreover, they also know how to employ these anecdotes for maximum effectiveness. They know how to read the collective mind of their audience based on the reaction that an anecdote provokes, and they also know how to adjust the anecdote itself based on that reaction.

Within the general category of the anecdote, a speaker can choose from several subclassifications. For example, if you are most comfortable with an informal style, you might want to make use of what's called an aside. This is a seemingly casual departure from the path of your speech—a departure that gains power from seeming spontaneous and unplanned. Abraham Lincoln, according to many reports, was a master of the aside. Again and again Lincoln would pause in his presentation of some crucial point and veer off in a new direction—usually remarking, "That reminds me of a story." The aside is a great attention getter. It works best when you feel that the concentration of the audience seems to be waning. If your listeners have been working hard to follow your train of thought, they'll respond to a humorous aside just as a marathon runner responds to a drink of water. You can reinvigorate them before returning to your main points. What's more, if it's done correctly, the aside will dovetail nicely into the body of your speech. You can even pretend to be surprised by this, especially if you've secretly spent hours practicing it in your hotel room.

One of the most useful categories of anecdotes is called the blunder story. This is just what it sounds like: you tell a story about some humorous mistake you made. By so doing, you gain not only the affection and the sympathy of your audience, but their admiration as well. They like you because you're a fallible human being, they feel sorry for you because you made a human mistake, and they admire you because you're able to admit it.

But let's look a little more closely at the blunder story, because with a few small adjustments you can make it especially effective. At one time, people might have laughed hardest at huge blunders. Some pain and even cruelty was thought to be essential for humor. A blunder that caused a house to burn down or a ship to sink would have people rolling in the aisles. But a modern blunder story works very differently. As any viewer of *Seinfeld* will tell you, the key today is basing your blunder on the *smallest* possible premise. We think it's much funnier to lose the cap to a tube of toothpaste than to slip on a banana peel in front of the queen of England. It's also much easier to find small-premise stories in our own lives. So give some thought to little things in your life that have gone awry, and see how they can be turned into humorous anecdotes in the *Seinfeld* manner. As Jerry Seinfeld himself said, it was supposed to be a show in which nothing happened. But really it was a show in which what happened was as close to nothing as possible, and that's what made it funny. By keeping that concept in mind, you'll find plenty of humorous material in the things that happen to you every day.

I hope all this sounds good to you. I hope it even sounds funny. But now let's face an ugly possibility. Suppose you're up in front of an audience and you've told anecdotes and you've veered off into asides and you've talked about losing the cap to the tube of toothpaste—and none of it has worked. It's just not funny. You know it and they know it. If that happens, congratulations, because you've opened up one of the most fertile fields of contemporary humor. Consider this: The talk show is one of the most original creations of American popular culture. It was born with the introduction of television, and it's still developing and changing today. But through all of its existence, one specific joke has been worked and reworked by every talk show host, up to and including Jay Leno and David Letterman. Quite simply, the joke is that the jokes aren't funny. From Steve Allen in the 1950s to Conan O'Brien in the twenty-first century, comedians have built careers on reacting to the audience's *failure* to laugh. By grimacing every time a line bombs, a comic is making the same joke over and over, a joke we can call recovery. If you do it right, it's a funny joke. So learn how to exploit your own vulnerability as a humorous speaker instead of hiding from it. Learn how to make the unfunniness of your material funny. Every speaker should attempt to master this basic aspect of contemporary humor.

The toolbox of humor has lots of implements. Maybe you've never thought about them analytically before—you just laughed when you thought something was funny. But by seeing the categories of humor, and by understanding which ones are closest to your personal style, you can maximize your ability to make people laugh.

However, this is another case of good news/bad news, and you know how funny those are. The good news is, you can definitely learn to recognize categories of humorous material and build an arsenal of funny stuff. The bad news is, you can have the funniest material in the world but you still have to deliver it effectively.

Good delivery is your ability to present humorous material in the best way possible. How many times have you heard a person tell a long, complicated anecdote, only to swallow the ending and ruin the story? The same thing can happen with a short joke or even a one-liner. Jokes and anecdotes are only the raw material. They have to be crafted to fit smoothly into your talk. Most important, they have to be congruent with the overall meaning of your presentation. Your humor can't be an end in itself. It has to reinforce the reason you're up in front of the audience, and your delivery has to show your understanding of that.

Effective speakers do not just play it for laughs. They use humor to illustrate their message. Chances are, you have been invited to educate and inform your audience. If you also wish to entertain them, it's because entertaining them will make you more successful in your primary task. A judicious use of humor in your talk will keep the audience on your side. But how much humor can an audience absorb in one talk? How many jokes or anecdotes can people hear before the humor becomes counter-productive? That question has no single answer because it all depends on your delivery.

To deliver humor well, your material needs to be practiced and perfected. Once you have found content that seems promising, the next step is to work on it in your mind. That doesn't mean you have to analyze it in an intellectual way—in fact, doing so is probably the quickest way to destroy any comic energy. Instead, learn to hear it inside your head. Then, just as with other aspects of your public-speaking material, practice delivering it out loud, both to yourself and to your friends. You'll learn something with every recitation.

Mark Twain said, "A humorous story can sometimes be a work of high and delicate art, provided that an artist is telling it. But no art is absolutely necessary in telling a comical story. In fact, anybody can do it." This is certainly true, but even telling a simple joke does take some skill. Pace, intonation, and pauses are all critical elements that can make humor fly or flop, and mastering them in a specific story always requires trial and error. So don't try your humor on a full audience until you're sure you can do it well, based on numerous rehearsals. Then, once you've used it in a presentation and it worked, use it again as often as possible. Vary your delivery and the emphasis you give to one element or another.

Become conscious of the critical relationship between timing and comical effect. Timing is essentially the distance between the various parts of a story or a joke. It's the space between the setup and the payoff of humorous material. To help with this, watch professionals to see how they create just the right rhythm between the beginning, the middle, and the end of a story. Notice how the nature of an audience can influence effective timing. Young, energetic listeners will want a faster pace than a more relaxed and older crowd. So if you're speaking to college students, your timing ought to be different from what you would use in a presentation to a group of retirees.

The more you know about your audience, the more fine-tuned your humor can be. So find out all you can about their demographics, their interests, their political leanings, their favorite sports teams—everything you possibly can. Every organization or group has its own history that can be studied. Procedures, rituals, and select individuals can be fertile ground for humor. Talk to the event planners and longtime members of the organization. Then consider the specific nature of the event. An awards ceremony for example—with the serious purpose of recognizing those who have accomplished great things—might not be well served by a humorous presentation. A technical-paper presentation might not seem a place for laughs, but perhaps some laughs will be needed precisely because of the dry subject matter. With practice and experience, you'll learn to make correct judgments in these areas, and your stature as a public speaker will grow as a result.

Some people say, "I could never use humor in my speech; I just don't feel comfortable with it." But anyone can use humor and every speaker should learn to employ this powerful tool. So in closing, let's review some of the key principles you'll want to keep in mind.

First, make sure the humor seems appropriate to the situation and funny to you. If you don't think something is funny, you certainly can't expect an audience to think so. That may seem so obvious that it doesn't even deserve mentioning, but it's amazing how many speakers ignore this basic premise. They fall back on worn-out, conventional material that would never make them laugh, but it seems safe, so they use it. That's a big mistake. Just as a salesperson should never sell a product that he or she wouldn't use, you should never tell a joke that wouldn't make you laugh.

Second, before using humor in a speech, try it out with a friend or with a small group of people. Even if your experimental group doesn't initially respond, don't give up too quickly. The problem might be in your delivery. Feeling at home with a funny story can take time. You should use humor in a speech only after you're comfortable telling it and have tested it repeatedly.

Third, make sure the humor relates to the content of your presentation. Humor should not be an end in itself. Making your audience laugh is a good thing, but it's not the primary reason you're there. If you don't tie your humor to your key theme, the audience may like the jokes, but they'll wonder what point you are attempting to make.

Finally, be careful that your humor doesn't come to dominate your identity behind the podium. You want to be known as a high impact public speaker, not as a comedian. Humor should be only one of many elements you weave into your presentations. If your speaking personality becomes dominated by the humorous element, an audience may have trouble relating to you when you tackle a serious subject.

Many efforts have been made to identify exactly what makes people laugh. If anyone comes up with the definitive answer, that person will make a fortune. But you don't need to be a philosopher of humor to use it in your presentations, and when you use it effectively, there is no more powerful tool for getting listeners on your side. The challenge is to use humor so that, if your audience remembers your jokes, they will also remember your message.

Few speeches which have produced an electrical effect on an audience can bear the colorless photography of a printed record.

—Archibald Philip Primrose

Liberty don't work as good in practice as it does in speeches.

—Will Rogers

Commencement oratory must eschew anything that smacks of partisan politics, political preference, sex, religion or unduly firm opinion. Nonetheless, there must be a speech: Speeches in our culture are the vacuum that fills a vacuum.

—John Kenneth Galbraith

CHAPTER 5

Stories and Self-Revelation:
How to Win Attention and Respect

G ood news! The information in this chapter can almost instantly transform you from a complete novice to a thoroughly professional speaker. So read it carefully, practice diligently, then start putting what you learn into action. Just by using the tools and techniques you'll gain here in chapter 5, you'll immediately be a more effective speaker than 99 percent of the people who are out there now.

To get started, let's imagine a retirement dinner in which two different guests are toasting the guest of honor. The first toast is given by the chief financial officer of the company. He says, "I always admired the acumen with which he managed his 401(k). He optimized his tax advantages to the greatest possible degree, and his account steadily increased in value every fiscal year." There is polite applause, and the financial officer sits down.

Then another colleague of the retiree's begins a toast. This person has known the guest of honor for many years. He describes the game in which his best buddy scored the only two points of his rather undistinguished basketball career. He says, "With seconds left in the game, he had the ball and an open path to the basket. But just then something really strange happened. He started to fall down, which was odd because there was nobody anywhere near him. It was as if he tripped over his own shoelace or something. In any case, he had to get rid of the ball before he hit the hardwood floor, so he just chucked it—and that was how he got his nickname, which as all of you know is Swish."

Both these men discussed the same topic: their friend. But they approached the topic in completely different ways. The topic of the first toast is difficult to visualize or dramatize. The second paints a picture of a specific incident, endows it with humor and drama, then connects it to the present as the origin of the subject's nickname. We learn something about the man who's retiring, but we also hear a story that's vivid. More than one thing is going on. In this chapter, we'll define the different elements of an effective speech, whether it's a toast at a small retirement dinner or an address to a large meeting of corporate shareholders.

In any high impact oral presentation, certain elements absolutely need to be present. The only exceptions would be simple PowerPoint talks or in small meetings in an office or a conference room. At all other times—whenever you're called upon to get up in front of an audience and speak for twenty or thirty minutes—you need to have these elements in place.

First, you need to clearly communicate the information or message of your talk. You need to get your facts and figures across. You need to have a theme or a thesis, and it has to be presented clearly and convincingly. This is why you are standing up there in the first place, yet in terms of the impact you will make, this is actually the least important part of your speech. Nobody will remember this aspect of your talk unless the other elements are at a home-run level. Your information is important, but information without impact disappears quickly from people's minds. So let's move ahead to the next of the key elements.

Element number two is stories or anecdotes about people *other than yourself.* In the previous chapter we discussed how an audience needs to laugh—not just *wants* to laugh, but *needs* to laugh—and they also *need* to hear stories. So if all you do is give them information, you don't fulfill one of your listeners' basic needs, and you're not doing your job as a speaker.

What kinds of stories should you tell? The answer to that depends on your levels of confidence and ability. A truly professional speaker makes every presentation a complete intellectual and emotional experience. That means the audience both thinks and feels—and with regard to feeling, the audience both *laughs and cries.*

Think about some of the best speakers you've ever heard. How did you feel at the end of their talks? I suspect you felt as if you'd traversed a full range of your emotions, all the way from laughter to tears. A good presenter can do this, and effective use of stories is a key tool for creating a full range of experiences for the reader. We spoke in the last chapter of Abraham Lincoln's ability to ease his audience into a humorous story. I suspect that Lincoln was able to do the same thing with narratives of many different kinds. I also suspect that Lincoln was effective partly because his speeches were not primarily for storytelling. His audiences had come to hear a political oration or a debate. They could buy into Lincoln's stories partly because those stories were a departure, and possibly even a relief.

You can present a wide variety of materials in virtually any presentation, and you should take full advantage of that. When you make a point about your central thesis, always see if you can link it to a story. Whenever you make people *think*, immediately follow up by making them *feel*. As your confidence grows, you'll be able to take listeners into a wider and wider range of feelings. People really want this from you as a speaker, even if they're not consciously aware of it.

Certain kinds of stories seem to succeed over and over. They work because people can identify with the situations and with the thoughts and emotions that go with them. Stories about airplanes and airports are always good. Most people like to travel and find it stimulating. But the hassles that come with air travel today are a good counterpoint to the excitement. Stories about families and children are also effective. Almost every parent has been on a long car trip with the kids in the backseat, so this is a ready-made setting for a story. If you want to tell a story about climbing Mount Everest, you'll have to spend some time painting the picture, but if you want to instantly connect with your audience, all you have to do is imitate your child saying, "Are we there yet?"

Regardless of the subject or the setting, good speakers never tell a story just for its own sake. It has to be relevant to the topic of the speech. It has to illustrate a point. As Dale Carnegie put it, stories are the frosting on the cake, not the cake itself. To extend the metaphor, stories are one of the two layers of the cake that we've discussed so far. The first layer, you'll recall, is the information content of your presentation, and the second is the narratives you use to illustrate your thesis. You'll also recall that these stories should be about someone other than yourself. That's because the next element we're going to look at is self-revelation—and how you can use it to make your speech a completely satisfying experience for your readers.

Although most stories are perceived as entertainment, they can also serve as a trigger for your audience to think and reflect. This is exactly what they should do. The success of your speech lies in the inner changes you bring about in your audience. We've seen how telling stories about other people can be a valuable tool in this respect. But telling about yourself—*revealing* yourself and the real challenges you've faced—might be even more essential.

This has to be done carefully, however. Remember, the key insight of the Dale Carnegie organization is that people's favorite topic is themselves. Chances are that you share this preoccupation with your own experiences. That can provide great energy for narratives of your personal experience, but somehow you will always have to relate it back to your audience.

In today's world, the bar has been set high in terms of how much people are willing to share about themselves. We live in a society that is used to Oprah and Dr. Phil, not to mention Judge Judy. You are not going to connect with your audience emotionally by confessing that you lost the cap to the toothpaste tube. We've seen how that exact confession can work well as a humorous anecdote, but what we're looking at here is a different layer of the cake. This is where you earn the audience's affection and their respect by the degree of risk you're willing to take. You earn their trust by trusting them with a part of yourself.

How far you should go with this depends on your own

comfort level as well as the setting in which your speech takes place. If you're leading a workshop on personal financial planning, you might want to reveal that you once maxed out your credit card—but you probably wouldn't talk about a health problem or a tragic situation in your family. Yet those concerns might be perfectly appropriate for an audience that expects an emotional connection.

In the financial planning workshop, for example, you might say something like "I began to wonder if I should look for a lower-interest credit card." But at a weekend retreat on personal transformation, nobody wants to hear about Visa or American Express. So now you'll say, "I began to wonder if I was wasting my life on unimportant things." You might even go further. You might say, "I had to take responsibility for the failure of my marriage."

A statement like that, with the self-revelation that it includes, may run the risk of offending some audiences. Such a statement might be too confrontational emotionally. By looking closely at yourself you are urging others to do the same, but what if they can't do that? They might just tune you out. That's why it's crucial always to spin every self-revelation story in a positive direction at the end. You can go as far as you dare into your own life's challenges, provided you connect with the positive changes that happened as a result.

Self-revelation is the most effective way to get into the hearts of your audience, which is different from getting into their minds. By sharing your personal experiences, you're letting them know that you are one of them. If you analyze any really powerful speech, you will always find a personal story embedded within it. Consider the Earl of Spencer's heartfelt eulogy for his sister, Princess Diana. With the entire world watching Diana's funeral, he said:

"The last time I saw her was in London on July first, her birthday. Typically, she was not taking time to celebrate her special day with friends but was instead at a fund-raising charity event. She was the sparkling guest of honor, of course, but I would rather cherish the days I spent with her in March when she came to visit me and my children in our home in South Africa. I am proud of the fact that apart from when she was on public display meeting President Mandela, we managed to contrive to prevent the photographers from getting a single picture of her. That meant a lot to Diana, and to me."

Notice how the speaker evokes the feeling of private family moments, even when he's describing one of the world's most public figures. In just a few lines, we get a sense of what Diana's feelings were, and of her brother's feelings as well. This is only a short section in a much longer talk, but without it the talk would be much less powerful.

The ability to create an intimate connection with their audience has always been a hallmark of great speakers. To appreciate this, and to learn how to do it yourself, you need to understand that a great speaker is always talking to only one person, no matter how vast the audience might actually be. Think of Franklin D. Roosevelt, who began making a series of radio broadcasts to the nation shortly after his first election as president. This was in 1933, during the worst of the Great Depression. The country needed leadership, but leadership with a gentle touch. Even the title that Roosevelt gave to his radio talks—they were called fireside chats—showed the president's genius for giving a human scale to a large enterprise.

First and most important, FDR visualized his audience as individuals, never as a mass of people. He knew his audience was hearing him one person at a time, so he spoke to them as if he were talking to a single person. You absolutely must do this to create a personal connection. You should visualize a single person who will represent the whole audience. Make up a story about that person's life. What are the challenges and the opportunities? What are the wants and the needs? The more specific you are about your listener, the more you will be able to connect. Do you know the color of her eyes? What is she wearing? Where does she live? What is her education? What is her financial status? There are dozens of questions like this—and you should have answers for all of them.

Assure yourself that your imaginary listener is receptive to your message. It's someone sympathetic to your cause and who has come to you for help. No matter how large your audience might actually be—even if it's a media-generated audience of thousands of people—speak to this single person. With practice, you will learn to transpose the face of your prototype onto any group of listeners.

Roosevelt sometimes imagined this person sitting with him on a porch or, even better, at a dinner table. This visualization created a feeling of intimacy and trust. Even though he was speaking into a radio microphone, his tone of voice and his facial expressions were those of an intimate friend. A frown on your face will make your voice sound harsh and cold, but a smile will make you sound warm and inviting. The president's face would light up as if he were actually sitting beside the fireplace with his listener. People sensed this, and it created a powerfully affectionate bond.

As he spoke, FDR's hands would move in simple, natural gestures. Most people think that good communication depends on the mouth, but that's much too limited. A powerful communicator uses his or her entire body. By using these techniques, you create a setting in which emotions can be shared naturally and gracefully. You've created the basis for the kind of self-revelation that is a hugely valuable element of good public speaking. By the time you're done with your presentation, your listeners should feel as if they know you. They don't have to know everything—it's always a good idea to let people use their imagination to some extent—but many of the basic facts should be shared. Where did you grow up? What was your family like when you were a child? What is your family like now? Are you single or married? If you have children, sharing a story about them is a great opportunity for connection with all the other parents in the audience.

I think you can see that using stories effectively is complex. You need to be intuitive, but you also need to be rational. You need to balance genuine emotion with correct decisions about how to use it. You need to be sincere, but you also need to be smart. By arousing your own emotions as a speaker, you can bring out the same emotions in your audience. But all this must happen within certain tactical guidelines. These are like the net and lines on a tennis court. They're the limits that give meaning to the emotional content of your speech. Without a net and lines, a great serve in tennis isn't a serve at all. It's just somebody hitting the ball hard. In the same way, emotional stories in a speech need to have a rational context and organization.

Let's look at some key tactics that should always be employed, regardless of how emotionally engaging your presentation might become. In all public speaking, and especially in storytelling, you are constantly making choices. You're making emotional choices, but you're also making rational decisions about, for example, using one word rather than another. These are not always easy decisions, and many speakers make the wrong ones.

When it comes to choosing your words, two rules are essential. The first is economy. That means using the fewest number of words to say what you want to say. If you have a point that can be made in ten words, don't use twenty. Don't even use twelve. In fact, see if you can use only eight. Anything that contributes to muddy, convoluted thought needs to go. Sometimes the hardest thing to do is to lose phrases you like, but if they don't contribute to your main theme, they must go.

You probably heard this same advice from your third-grade English teacher. But here's something you probably didn't know, and you should never forget it if you intend to be a high impact speaker. You need to use the fewest possible number of words in a sentence because you will have to repeat a variation of that sentence at least twice, or even three times. This is a basic difference between written and spoken language. If you are writing a book, your words are fixed on the page for readers to see. If they don't understand exactly what you mean, they can and should read the words again. But a live audience doesn't have that option. Your words are there for an instant, then are gone. There's no playback in real-time speech. So whether it's a description in a story or a point of information, you must find a way to convey the same message more than once. You must also do it in the most concise and hard-hitting way. That's why the fewest number of words possible in any sentence is absolutely the way to go.

But that's just the beginning. You should not only use the *fewest* possible words, but also the *simplest* possible words. Overestimating the vocabulary of your audience is a big mistake, because you risk losing their attention immediately. When Ronald Reagan, known as the Great Communicator, addressed Mikhail Gorbachev, he didn't say, "Comrade General Secretary, in this instant I demand that this geopolitical mortar-and-metaphorical hindrance be retracted." He said, "Mr. Gorbachev, tear down this wall." Keep that example in mind and you'll never have problems with the level of your vocabulary.

Whenever you tell a story or share personal information about yourself, be sure that the connection to the overall theme of your speech is explicit and will not offend even one member of the audience. There are several reasons for this. It's possible, for example, that your stories are so engaging that listeners will forget the real purpose of your talk. Or if the stories are something less than engaging, the audience may simply lose focus. So maintain connection to your theme through emphasis and repetition at appropriate moments. When Martin Luther King Jr. spoke at the Lincoln Memorial, he repeated one sentence: "I have a dream." Even if we're not certain about what he said in between, we remember his repeating that theme again and again. This was his basic point, and he made sure that it would not be forgotten.

Something else that's important is to use props whenever you have an opportunity. Hold something up for the audience to see. Play a brief recording or project an image onto a screen. Remember show-and-tell in grammar school? "Tell" was almost always the boring part. What we wanted was to actually see the pet turtle—so give your audience something beyond the experience of just listening to your voice. Even if you don't have a turtle to show them, you can use gestures and body language to add a visual dimension to your talk. Use physical energy to show that you yourself are interested in your topic. Don't just stand there. Make your speech a visual as well as an audio experience. This is the difference between reading a speech and true public speaking.

Watch your *ums* and *uhs*. Most people don't realize how often these wasted syllables intrude in their oral communication, especially when they're speaking in front of an audience. *Um* and *uh* are expressions of nervousness. They're unconscious ways of buying time because you're not certain of what you're going to say next. So the more prepared you are, the less nervous you'll be, and the less you'll need to stall. You should always speak warmly, but your voice should also convey focus and deliberation. Oprah Winfrey is one of the best in the world at this. She always seems interested, excited, but focused and under control. This makes the audience feel exactly the same way.

There's so much to say about getting the audience on your side that this one chapter could be an entire book by itself. We've spoken about the need to communicate the basic themes and information of your talk, and we've also discussed the importance of creating an emotional connection with the audience. We've seen two ways to make this connection: the first is with stories about other people; the second is by sharing information about yourself. These are your tools for winning the respect and affection of your audience. We've also discussed practical tactics for maximizing your impact, such as choosing the right vocabulary and employing eye-catching visual aids.

But all these are a means to an end. Any good speaker wants more than just the attention and affection of the audience. A good public speaker wants to inspire *action*. We'll explore how to do that in chapter 6.

Eleanor Roosevelt

Excerpt from Eleanor Roosevelt's "Struggle for Human Rights" speech, September 28, 1948, Paris, France:

> *I have come this evening to talk with you on one of the greatest issues of our time—that is the preservation of human freedom. I have chosen to discuss it here in France, at the Sorbonne, because here in this soil the roots of human freedom have long ago struck deep and here they have been richly nourished. It was here the Declaration of the Rights of Man was proclaimed, and the great slogans of the French Revolution—liberty, equality, fraternity—fired the imagination of men. I have chosen to discuss this issue in Europe because this has been the scene of the greatest historic battles between freedom and tyranny. I have chosen to discuss it in the early days of the General Assembly because the issue of human liberty is decisive for the settlement of outstanding political differences and for the future of the United Nations.*

President Franklin Roosevelt was a magnificent orator, but when he became too severely disabled to travel around the country giving political speeches, he turned to his wife, Eleanor, to speak on his behalf. Eleanor was extremely bright and well-spoken, but she had an overwhelming terror of public speaking. Her husband had said in a famous speech, "The only thing we have to fear is fear itself," and Eleanor took that to heart, looked her fear straight in the face, conquered it, and became the greatest female public speaker of her time.

In her book *You Learn by Living*, Eleanor Roosevelt urged her readers not to cower before the world's dangers, but to stare them down, as she did her fear of public speaking: "You gain strength, courage and confidence by every experience in which you really stop to look fear in the face. . . . You must do the thing which you think you cannot do."

The thing that Eleanor Roosevelt thought she could not do—public speaking—became one of things she did best. She gave speeches all over the world on a wide variety of topics.

On V-J Day

The day for which the people of the world have prayed is here at last. There is great thankfulness in our hearts. Peace has not come, however, as the result of the kind of power which we have known in the past, but as the result of a new discovery which as yet is not fully understood, nor even developed.

On civil rights

We have a great responsibility here in the United States because we offer the best example that exists perhaps today throughout the world, of the fact that if different races know each other they may live peacefully together.

On the Pearl Harbor attack

Good evening, ladies and gentlemen, I am speaking to you tonight at a very serious moment in our history. The Cabinet is convening and the leaders in Congress are meeting with the President. The State Department and Army and Navy officials have been with the President all afternoon. In fact, the Japanese ambassador was talking to the President at the very time that Japan's airships were bombing our citizens in Hawaii and the Philippines and sinking one of our transports loaded with lumber on its way to Hawaii.

On the arts

I think that we all of us now are conscious of the fact that the appreciation of beauty is something which is of vital importance to us, but we are also conscious of the fact that we are a young country, and we are a country that has not had assurance always in its own taste.

On pensions for the elderly

I do not feel that I have to discuss the merits of old age pensions with my audience. It is many years now since we have accepted the fact, I think, pretty well throughout the country, that it is the right of old people when they have worked hard all their lives, and, through no fault of theirs, have not been able to provide for their old age, to be cared for in the last years of their lives.

Today's public figures can no longer write their own speeches or books, and there is some evidence that they can't read them either.

—Gore Vidal

Commencement speeches were invented largely in the belief that outgoing college students should never be released into the world until they have been properly sedated.

—G. B. Trudeau

The best way to sound like you know what you're talking about is to know what you're talking about.

—Author unknown

CHAPTER 6

Motivating Your Listeners to Action

A good public speaker is just like the captain of a ship. A ship has a direction and a destination. The captain is always aware of the destination and is also aware of where the ship is at every moment in relation to the final objective. Ask the commanders of any ocean liners where they're going, and they can tell you instantly—and in one sentence.

How many speakers can do the same thing? Most of them want to accomplish many different things, or at least they think they want them. As a result, they're unable to focus their efforts, their minds, and their hearts on anything specific. All this leads to doubt and confusion, first in the speakers themselves and then in their audience. They don't recognize how vital it is to pick one port that's important and then sail to it. But if you can learn how to do this, you can set and reach goals for each of your presentations, one by one, until eventually you will have a list of accomplishments as a speaker in which to take pride.

Oddly, sometimes speakers have quite the opposite problem. Instead of not knowing where the ship is bound, the ship isn't going anywhere at all. The speech seems to be in dry dock and could stay there until falling apart from rust and disuse. A ship's engine isn't started until she has some place to go. It's the same with an oral presentation. This is why it's so important for every talk to have a port of call the speaker wants to reach—a goal—a place to get to where the audience will feel better than in the place it now finds itself. If the speaker has no clear objective, the presentation might never cast off. The engines might never start, and the audience will never know the thrill of sailing a charted course to a destination that gradually emerges in the journey.

If someone stopped you in the middle of a presentation and asked what your next port of call is—that is, where exactly you are headed in your talk—could you answer in one simple sentence, as could the captain on the bridge of his ship? If not, maybe you should give that some thought. Of course, the time to do that isn't while a speech is in progress. The best time is long before that. If you have a presentation scheduled in the near future, the best time might be right now.

When you think about yourself as a public speaker, what aspect of your presentations would you most like to strengthen? Would you like to impart your ideas more clearly? Or do you want to touch the emotions of your listeners more deeply? But before you choose your answer, let me ask one even more important question. As a speaker, why do you want to have greater intellectual or emotional impact? Why do you want to be a speaker in the first place? This time, there's no need to respond at all, because the answer is obvious. You want to move your listeners to action. You intend for them to make something happen based on what they've heard. You don't want them to say, "That was a lovely speech." You want them to say, "Let's march!"

A speech or presentation is given in public for only three

basic reasons: to inform, to entertain, or to inspire action. Inspiring action is by far the most frequent, the most important, and the most challenging motive. Bringing about action on the part of your listeners is not a matter of blind luck, nor is it simply a talent that certain speakers have and others lack. It is a *skill* that can be learned and mastered. Intelligent, clearly defined methods exist for learning that skill, as you're about to discover.

The first step is gaining the interest, the attention, and the confidence of your listeners. We've spoken about this in earlier chapters. Unless you achieve those basic goals—especially winning the confidence of the audience—listeners can have no faith in what you say.

The best way to win confidence is to show you deserve it. In an oral presentation, this means more than just deploying lots of facts and figures. Regarding this, Dale Carnegie liked to quote J. Pierpont Morgan, one of the wealthiest men in the world at the start of the twentieth century. Morgan said that just as character was the biggest element in obtaining credit from a bank, the perception of your character is also crucial for obtaining the confidence of your audience. You've probably noticed this yourself. Glib, witty speakers are not nearly as effective as those who are less brilliant but more sincere.

In a Dale Carnegie class on public speaking, one student had a truly striking appearance, and when he stood up to talk, he showed amazing fluency of thought and language. But when he finished, most people simply remarked how clever he was or how impressive he looked onstage. He made a good impression on the surface, but it was on the surface only.

In that same class was a woman who worked as an insurance

representative. She was short, she sometimes groped for a word, and she lacked graceful self-expression. But deep sincerity shone in her eyes and vibrated in her voice. People naturally listened closely to what she said. Without even being conscious of why, they instinctively had faith in her, and as a result they were ready to put her ideas into action in their own lives.

For a speaker, sincerity is the wild card that trumps everything else. Deep, genuine sincerity is the first characteristic of all credible presenters. No audience can deny the truth of emotions that you feel at a deep level, nor would any audience *care* to deny them. On the contrary, they want to feel what you're sincerely feeling. They want to share the experiences of your life for the few moments that you're standing before them.

To give an audience that gift, you must first give it to yourself. You need to open up to your feelings before you can invite others in. Often, particularly in highly emotional or stressful situations, people look for ways to escape the true challenge of the moment. They rely on what they think they're supposed to feel instead of what's really in their hearts. If you can avoid that trap and be totally honest with yourself, you'll discover a vast resource of feelings that you can share with your listeners. Your sincerity will be obvious, and sincerity is the first and best way to gain the trust and confidence of your listeners.

The essence of this is the ability to ground your message in your personal life experience. If you just give your opinions, people may counter them with their own. If your speech just relates what you've heard or repeats what you've read, it will always have a secondhand flavor. But what you yourself have gone through and lived through will ring genuine. The truth of it isn't just your opinion, it's your history, and it's your life.

Since you're the world's leading authority on that topic, your audience can't help but believe you.

There's no need to go it alone when it comes to winning the confidence of an audience. Many speakers make this difficult for themselves simply because they haven't been properly introduced. The English word *introduction* links two words from Latin: *intra*, which means "to the inside," and *ducere* (pronounced "*duke*-airy"), meaning "to lead." An introduction to an idea ought to lead us into the topic so that we want to hear it discussed. And an introduction to a speaker should lead us to the inside facts regarding him or her, facts that demonstrate the speaker's fitness for discussing a particular subject. An introduction ought to "sell" both the topic and the speaker to the audience. And it ought to do this as forcefully and economically as possible.

That is what an introduction ought to do. But nine times out of ten that isn't what happens. Dale Carnegie saw this firsthand when he heard an introduction for the great Irish poet William Butler Yeats, who was going to read from his own poetry. Just three years earlier Yeats had been awarded the Nobel Prize in literature, the highest distinction that can be bestowed upon a man of letters. Yet not 10 percent of the audience knew of that award, or of Yeats's stature in the world of letters. Both of these should have been mentioned in the introduction. They should have been announced even if nothing else was said.

But the master of ceremonies completely ignored these facts. Instead, he wandered off into his own thoughts on mythology and Greek poetry. No doubt he was entirely unconscious that his ego was prompting him to impress the audience with his knowledge and importance. He actually was quite important, internationally known as a speaker, and had been introduced a thousand times himself. With this in mind, Dale Carnegie saw exactly what was happening. This person's own stature made him a total failure at elevating the stature of another person.

If that can happen to a Nobel Prize–winning writer, how can you prevent it from happening to you? Well, it just requires a bit of diplomacy. So with all due humility of soul, go to the person who will introduce you and provide some information. Your suggestions will be greatly appreciated. Indicate the points you would like to have mentioned, points that show why you are qualified to talk about this particular subject. These are the simple facts that the audience ought to know, and that will win you an attentive hearing. It's even a good idea to write these points on an index card, so the introducer can refer to them in the best possible way.

We've spoken about the importance of sincerity in connecting with your audience. Another quality—let's call it *earnestness*—is related to sincerity but is also different from it. To make this distinction clear, Dale Carnegie liked to tell the following story.

When Mr. Carnegie was conducting courses in public speaking in New York City, one of the city's star salesmen took the course. During a practice talk he made a preposterous statement about being able to grow blue grass. He said he had scattered wood ashes over newly plowed ground, and the grass that grew in had simply turned out blue. He firmly asserted that the ashes alone were responsible for the blue grass.

In discussing the salesman's talk, Dale Carnegie pointed out that this phenomenon, if true, would instantly earn a unique place in the history of botany, and maybe of science in general. It might even make the speaker a great deal of money—because no other person, living or dead, had ever been able to perform this remarkable feat.

Dale Carnegie also pointed out, however, that what the speaker said was completely unbelievable. There was no need even to take the time to refute it, because everyone already saw the truth.

But the speaker doggedly stuck to his guns. He was earnest about his contention. He leaped to his feet and proclaimed the truth of what he'd said. He had not been relating theory, after all, but his personal experience. He knew whereof he spoke. He gave additional information, piled up additional evidence. A fierce sincerity and honesty shone through his voice.

Again, Mr. Carnegie informed him that he could not in the remotest possibility in the world be telling the truth, or even be within a thousand miles of the truth. Well, in a second he was on his feet once more, offering to let the Department of Agriculture settle the matter. He was willing to bet a large amount of money on the outcome.

Dale Carnegie now noticed something surprising. The salesman had clearly won over several members of the course. Marveling at their credulity, Mr. Carnegie asked why they had now come to believe in the possibility of blue grass. The class members all gave the same explanation. It was the earnestness of the speaker. He could not have been so earnest and enthusiastic about something unless it was the truth.

The power of earnestness is incredible, especially with an audience that is relatively uninformed about the topic. For better or for worse, few people have the capacity for hard-minded, logical thought. But all of us have feelings and emotions, and all of us can be influenced by a speaker's feelings. If the speaker believes a thing earnestly enough and says it earnestly enough, even though the claim is preposterous, he or she will gain adherents and win disciples. The speaker will gain the confidence of the listeners simply by virtue of having so much confidence.

Once the hurdle of gaining confidence has been surmounted, the work of translating this into action begins. Now you must state the facts that will educate people on the merits of your proposition. This is the heart of your talk. This is where your preparation will count. Now you will want to know many times more about your topic than you can possibly use. In regard to this, Dale Carnegie liked to use an example from Lewis Carroll's sequel to *Alice's Adventures in Wonderland*, entitled *Through the Looking Glass*. When the White Knight in *Through the Looking Glass* started out on his journey, he prepared for every possible contingency. He took a mousetrap in case he was troubled with mice at night, and he carried a beehive in case he found a stray swarm of bees. Well, if the White Knight had prepared speeches in the same way, he would have been a winner. He would have been able to overwhelm any resistance with a torrent of information. He would have been more than ready for any objection that could possibly appear. He would have known his subject so well, and planned his talk so thoroughly, that anything but success was impossible.

Here's an example of how this works. The CEO of a manufacturing firm realized that it was necessary to raise the price of some of its core products. His sales managers protested. They said there would be a huge loss of business, and that prices had to be kept where they were. So the CEO called a national meeting. He stood before his sales force with a large sheet of paper on the wall behind him.

One by one, the CEO asked his salespeople to state their objections to the increase in prices—and the objections came like shots from a machine gun. As fast as they came, the CEO noted them on the big sheet of paper. The entire morning was spent in that way. The meeting adjourned with at least a hundred different reasons listed why prices should not be raised. Every possible reason was up there on the wall, and for most of those present the issue must have seemed conclusively settled.

That afternoon, however, the CEO refuted all of those objections. He could only do this because he had thought of every single one of them beforehand. Nothing surprised him. He was totally prepared. No loose ends were left. Everything was settled on the spot.

But as impressive as this is, for our purposes in this chapter it's not really enough. A meeting like that with a sales force should end with something more than all of them nodding their heads. A meeting of salespeople should break up with the attendees filled with new enthusiasm. They have to be ready not just for agreement, but for action as well. To make that happen, refuting objections is an important step but not the critical one. That critical step is to appeal to the motives that make people act.

We can understand this in terms of cause and effect. The world and everything in it are run not haphazardly, but according to the immutable laws of cause and effect. Everything that ever *has* happened or ever *will* happen is the logical and inevitable effect of something that preceded it. It is also the logical cause of something that will follow. So what is the first cause of every action? What brings about every conscious and deliberate act we perform? The answer is one word. *Desire.*

The things that we desire are not many. Hour by hour, day and night, we are influenced by a surprisingly small number of longings. So if you as a speaker can learn what these motives are and can appeal to them with sufficient force, you will have extraordinary power. The wise speaker attempts to do exactly that.

Suppose, for example, that a father finds that his teenage son has surreptitiously been smoking cigarettes. Naturally, the father might grow irate. He might warn his son—or even threaten him—that smoking will ruin his health.

The trouble is, few teenagers fear ruined health. They're much more in touch with the adventure of breaking a rule than with fear of long-term physical consequences. What will happen here? Probably nothing good—because the father was not shrewd enough to play upon a desire that touched his son. Instead, the father used only the desire that he *himself* responded to.

The father would have a lot more success if he could get outside his own feelings and over to the boy's side of the fence. Maybe his son wants success in sports, but smoking makes him winded after even a short run. Maybe he wants popularity with girls. Maybe he would like to spend his money on something other than cigarettes. All these desires could negatively be affected by smoking. All of them could also be called upon by the father in getting his son to stop. It's a matter of meeting the listener where he really is in life, instead of where you think he ought to be or where you are yourself.

A powerful tactic can be put to work here. High impact speakers know how to get action by setting one desire against another. If a teenager wants to smoke, we need to ask what he wants *even more* than smoking. Then we can use that desire to create a connection. You can always use certain basic human desires to shape the conduct of your listeners. Understanding these universal desires and molding them is essential to the success of a public speaker, so we need to see exactly what they are.

One of the strongest of these desires is for personal gain. This is the reason why a few hundred million people get out of bed every morning two or three hours earlier than they otherwise would. But powerful as this desire is, an even stronger motive is self-protection. For most people making money is a fine aspiration, but not losing money is an absolute necessity. To appeal to this motive most strongly, make it personal.

Returning to the example of smoking, quoting statistics about future lung disease is not the best tactic. Instead, show what the cost will be *today*. The proximity in time is much more important than the severity of the loss. If a young man is turned down for a date because of smoking, the impact will be far greater than that of the vision of himself on a respirator forty years from now. That might be an unfortunate fact of human nature, but it is a fact nonetheless.

So we have seen that desire for gain is a strong motive for action, and we've also seen that fear of loss is even stronger. But one of Dale Carnegie's greatest insights is the realization that even these impulses are not the strongest human motives. They pale in comparison to what Mr. Carnegie called *pride*, and which could be more exactly expressed as *the wish to be admired*. That's what pride means in terms of the will to action. As Dale Carnegie put it, the appeal to pride, if done skillfully, has a force only a trifle less potent than dynamite's.

Ask yourself why you are reading this book. Were you moved by the wish to make a better impression in your presentations? Did you covet the glow of inward satisfaction that comes from making a highly effective talk? Won't you feel a very pardonable pride in the power, leadership, and distinction naturally accorded to the public speaker?

Human beings are creatures of feeling who long for physical comfort and pleasures. But the physical dimension of that longing is relatively superficial. Few people buy an expensive automobile in order to keep it in the garage and sit on the leather seats. They want to be out and about so they can be seen in the car. Why has physical fitness become such an obsession with the American public? Millions of people aren't going to the gym so that they can run better times in the marathon. They're doing it so that they can look good at the beach on weekends or even on the street every day.

We've used Abraham Lincoln as an example of a great public speaker. But Lincoln was also a human being, and for most of his life he was in the public eye. So why did he grow a beard? Was it because he got tired of shaving so often? Was it because he wanted to look distinguished to himself when he looked in the mirror every morning? No—it was because someone confided to him that with a beard he would look more authoritative in the eyes of other people. He would have greater credibility. He would be more *admired*.

Lincoln was six feet four inches tall. That was an enormous height in an era when the average height for a man was about five feet seven. Yet Lincoln wore a top hat that made him look even taller. He was a great man and a humble man at the core of his being, yet even Lincoln wanted to be admired and to stand out in a crowd. It's just a basic element of human nature, and appealing to this basic element is the best way to inspire action in an audience.

So as you're getting ready for a presentation, ask yourself these questions: What can you offer your listeners that will raise the admiration they'll get from the people that are important to them? Who will be proud of the salesman when he meets his monthly quota? Who will write a letter to the human resources executive when a dispute is successfully resolved? If you think about it, you will always be able to find some *external* audience that *your own* audience wants to please. Once you've made that determination, show your listeners exactly what actions they need to take to obtain that recognition. If you've done your job well, you can rest assured that they will indeed take those actions. If you've connected those actions to the basic themes of your speech, your talk will be a complete success.

In closing, let's review the steps we've covered during this critical chapter. First, we've seen that public speaking is not just a rhetorical exercise. It may have been that in the time of the ancient Greeks, but today speaking is not an end in itself. It's not just about what goes through people's heads when they're sitting in the room listening to you. It's not even about what they feel in their hearts. It *is* about what happens when they get up and start walking around again. As a speaker, you want them to go in the direction you point them in.

Next, we saw that you can use certain basic principles and tools to achieve this goal. We saw the importance of connecting with what our listeners really want, not just what we think they ought to want. Those motives might not be as lofty as you would wish, but you need to meet people where they are to get them to where you think they ought to be. Great speakers have always understood this and used it for their benefit. Only mediocre speakers choose to fight against the realities of human nature.

Third, we discussed the importance of gaining the confidence of your audience. Win their confidence by deserving it—by your sincerity, by being properly introduced, by being qualified to speak on your subject, by sharing evidence and information that your own experience has taught you. We saw also that earnestness can be a powerful tool for confidence building, even when you're facing skeptical listeners.

Then muster as many facts as possible to support your assertion. Be prepared for every possible objection. The better prepared you are for objections, the less chance you'll ever have to deal with them. This is a mysterious fact about public speaking, but it's true nonetheless.

Finally and most important, connect with the desire for gain, the need for self-protection, and the pride that people feel when they're admired by others. These are the universals that everyone experiences. The art of great public speaking lies in seeing how those universals express themselves in a specific audience in a given time and place.

The call to action is a specific goal for you as a public speaker, and I trust this chapter has provided equally specific tools for achieving it. In chapter 7 we'll confront how you have only a few minutes—a few seconds, really—to begin deploying these tools.

Public speaking is the art of diluting a two-minute idea with a two-hour vocabulary.

—Evan Esar

What this country needs is more free speech worth listening to.

—Hansell B. Duckett

There are two things that are more difficult than making an after-dinner speech: climbing a wall which is leaning toward you and kissing a girl who is leaning away from you.

—Winston Churchill

CHAPTER 7

Winning the First Minute: Making a Positive Impression

Ask professional speakers about the most valuable lessons they've learned, and you'll always hear the same response: "You need to start fast. You need a dynamic opening that gets the attention of the audience right off the bat."

To make this happen, great speakers know in advance the exact words they'll use in both the opening and closing of their talks. But does the beginner know this? Hardly ever, and that's a big mistake. Winning the first minute of a speech takes time, requires thought, and demands willpower. So don't take the easy way out. Force yourself to look carefully and clearly at what you're going to say in front of the audience. Know exactly what impression you want to make. Then come up with the words that will allow you to make that impression as quickly as possible.

Ever since the days of the ancient Greeks, oral presentations have been divided into three sections: the introduction, the body, and the conclusion. But what goes on during those three sections has dramatically changed. In ancient times, the introduction could be like a leisurely buggy ride. Speakers were both bringers of news and entertainers. People were in no hurry to get to the end of a speech because there weren't many other sources of diversion.

Today there seems to be nothing *but* diversion. The world has been remade by television, iPods, the Internet, and cell phones. More innovations have occurred in the last hundred years than since time began. For you as a speaker, this demands getting in sync with the impatient rhythm of the times. If you are going to use an introduction, it ought to be as short and flashy as a website banner. That's about all the modern audience can sit still for. You have to grab their attention immediately. Once you've done that you can proceed with your talk—but *only* if you've done that.

Martin Luther King Jr. was one of the greatest speakers of the twentieth century. He knew how to reach his audiences instantly. Read the opening of his famous "I Have a Dream" speech:

"Five score years ago, a great American, in whose symbolic shadow we stand today, signed the Emancipation Proclamation. This momentous decree came as a great beacon light of hope to millions of slaves who had been seared in the flames of withering injustice.

"But one hundred years later, the slaves are still not free."

No one can ignore an opening like that. No one can read the soaring cadences of those sentences and still think about his cell phone or his iPod. This doesn't mean you have to be a Martin Luther King Jr. to be an effective speaker, but you should definitely be aware of his example. By doing so, you can avoid the most common mistakes made by so many speakers day in and day out.

Average speakers generally open their talks in one of two

ways, both of which are wrong. The first mistake is to open with a humorous story. Since we've already devoted an entire chapter to humor, you know that this is an important element of a successful speech. But that doesn't mean it should be the first thing people hear. True, a well-known public figure with a reputation for being intimidating may want to break the ice with a joke. But if you're not Donald Trump, your immediate focus shouldn't be putting people at their ease. Your focus should be on getting their full attention and their respect. Once you've accomplished that, you can think about lightening the mood a bit. Remember, a good speech is like a sumptuous meal. Humor is the dessert, not the main course. Don't give it to people too soon because you think that's a quick way to win them over. It's really a quick way to lose them.

Starting out with humor is a way of trying to have the audience on your side without earning that privilege. It's an expression of insecurity, and so is the other most common opening mistake. It may sound hard to believe, but many speakers start out by apologizing for making a speech in the first place! They'll say things like "I am not a polished orator. . . . I am not really prepared for this talk. . . . I'm not sure that I really have anything to say"—and a dozen other variations on this theme.

Again, what's behind this is insecurity. You're convinced that the audience is going to criticize you, so you try to beat them to the punch by criticizing yourself. Don't do it! If you're not prepared, some listeners will know it soon enough without your help. Others will not even notice—so why call their attention to it? One thing is certain: no one wants to hear your preemptive apologies.

The moment you come before the audience, you automatically

have their attention, but only for a very, very brief time. You have a five-second grace period, but you need to extend this for at least the first five minutes. If you can successfully do that, you'll have won them over and you can move effectively into the body of your talk. But if you lose them at the start, it will be extremely difficult to win them back. So begin with something interesting in your very first minute. Not the second. Not the third. *The first!*

How should you go about this? It may seem like a large order, but some clear guidelines exist for you to follow.

Here's an opening that was used by one of the students in the Dale Carnegie public-speaking course. See if it gets your interest immediately.

"Eighty-two years ago, and just about this time of year, there was published in London a little story that was destined to become immortal. Many people have called it 'the greatest little book in the world.' When it first appeared, friends meeting one another on the street asked the question 'Have you read it?' The answer was always 'Yes, God bless him, I have.'

"The first day it was published, a thousand copies were sold. Within two weeks, the number was fifteen thousand. Since then there have been countless editions in dozens of languages. The original manuscript has been sold for a fabulous sum, and it now rests among other priceless treasures in a private library."

Do you consider that a successful opening? Does it hold your attention? Most readers feel that it does, and the reason is simple. It can be expressed in one word: *curiosity.* This opening works because it asks a question and then creates suspense about what the answer is going to be. The speaker isn't suggesting that the fate of the world is at stake, but as he keeps referring to the fabulous success of this book, you can't help but wonder what it is. But he doesn't tell you. He just keeps teasing you. Finally, after even more buildup, he reveals that the book is Charles Dickens's *A Christmas Carol*. But by then the work of the opening is done. He's kept the attention of the audience for the first few minutes, and now they're ready to receive the rest of the speech.

Curious interest is the key. In the words of Dale Carnegie, "Who is not susceptible to curiosity? I have seen birds in the woods fly about by the hour watching me out of sheer curiosity. I know a hunter in the high Alps who lures elk by throwing a bed sheet around himself and crawling around. In this way he arouses their curiosity. Dogs have curiosity, and so have kittens, and all manner of animals including the well-known genus *Homo sapiens.*"

When you arouse your audience's interest from the first minute, you can gain their undivided attention for at least an hour. The reason for this lies at the foundation of human nature. People are the most insatiably curious creatures on earth. But to engage that natural curiosity, speakers must know two things about their readers: First, what is the audience's present level of interest in a given topic? And second, what value can the speaker attach to the topic that will raise that interest to the point of taking action?

Let me illustrate this with an extremely hypothetical example. Suppose you were addressing a chamber of commerce or a local trade association. Suppose you began your talk with something like this: "Ladies and gentlemen, before I begin my talk, I have an important announcement to make. I've just been informed that a very wealthy philanthropist is giving away five-thousand-dollar checks to the first hundred entrepreneurs who request one. If anyone is curious about where this philanthropist can be found, just ask me and I will be happy to supply the address." Obviously, everyone present would immediately ask for the address; people are inherently interested in money. They're inherently curious about where they can get money with no effort on their part. They have a strong, hardwired interest in what you've just told them.

But now suppose that you'd said something very different before you mentioned that generous philanthropist. Suppose you had said, "Wealth depends on having an excellent vocabulary. So I strongly urge everyone to buy a dictionary and learn twenty new words each week." Because you have not made a clear connection between the hardwired desire for wealth and the idea that it depends on learning new words, you are probably not going to get bowled over by the crowd rushing off to Barnes & Noble. For that to happen, you would need to make the connection between what you've said and their interest much more explicit. If, for example, you offered a substantial cash award to anyone who could pass a difficult vocabulary test, you would immediately see a lot of people trying to learn the definition of words like *prestidigitator*.

Another example. A student opened an oral report by asking, "Do you know that slavery exists in seventeen nations of the world today?" This not only aroused curiosity, but also shocked his readers. "Slavery? Today? Seventeen countries? That seems incredible. What nations? Where are they?"

You can always arouse curiosity by beginning with an effect and making people want to hear the cause. Another student began a report with this striking statement: "A member of our state legislature recently proposed a law prohibiting tadpoles from becoming frogs within two miles of any schoolhouse."

You smile. Is the speaker joking? How absurd. Was that actually done? Yes, it was—and the speaker then explained what had happened.

A column on jobs and careers for *Fortune* magazine aroused curiosity with the question "Do people in your office seem less enthusiastic than they used to?" With twelve words the author announces the subject of the article and ignites readers' curiosity about why workers have lost their enthusiasm. Every aspiring public speaker ought to study the techniques that writers use to hook a reader's interest. You can learn much more this way than you can by studying collections of printed speeches.

In an earlier chapter we discussed the importance of using stories in your presentations. Although blatantly humorous stories are not a good way to start, other kinds of narratives can be extremely effective. From ancient times onward, storytellers have entertained, educated, and enlightened their readers. Troubadours sang ballads or recited poems and sagas of heroes. We still want and need to hear stories. We buy books and magazines, go to the theater and to movies, listen to the radio, and watch TV. Don't ignore this very human need. Work with it rather than against it. Exotic, travelogue-style openings are almost foolproof. They can't fail. They move, they march, and the audience follows. Plain and simple, listeners want to know what happens next.

What about this opening sentence, which is adventurous in a different way: "When men and women work together, there will likely be flirtations, romances, and even marriages. What problems does this present for a company?"

This opening starts the ball rolling with an open-ended question. The next step is to follow it up with a reality-based narrative. Tell a story about an office romance. Most people will find that difficult to ignore. Then you can go back to answer the question you began with.

Even a raw beginner can manage a successful opening by using a story to arouse curiosity. It's difficult or even impossible for an average audience to follow abstract statements for long. Narratives are much easier, so why not start with one? Yet many speakers resist that. They think that general statements are more serious and respectable than storytelling. In the first place, that's simply not true, and in any case it's best to go with what works, regardless of the philosophical validity. So open with your story, capture the interest, then proceed with your general remarks.

Probably the easiest way to gain instant attention is to give people something physical to look at. One Dale Carnegie student opened a talk by holding up a discount coupon and waving it above her head. Naturally everyone looked. Then she asked, "Has anyone here ever received a coupon like this in the mail? It announces that the recipient will be given a free boat ride and dinner and a tour of a beautiful new real estate development on the Hudson River. All he or she has to do is to call and present this coupon." That got their attention. She then revealed how this trick was used to entice people to the development so they could be exposed to a high-pressure sales pitch.

This student's opening has another great feature. It begins by asking a question that we know will get an affirmative answer. Everybody gets junk mail, so asking about it gets the audience thinking with the speaker and cooperating with her.

This question gambit is one of the simplest, surest ways to unblock the attention of your readers and let them hear what you have to say. To add a further spin to the question technique, why not open with a question posed by a famous person? The words of prominent people always have attention power, so a suitable quote is one of the best ways to launch a talk. Here's an example:

"Humanity is an ocean. If a few drops of the ocean are polluted, the ocean does not become dirty. So how can we lose faith in humanity because of the actions of a few human beings?"

This opening has several commendable features. The initial sentences arouse curiosity: why should we have faith in humanity? Then, after a skillful pause by the speaker, we learn the source of the quote: Mahatma Gandhi. The power of that name now carries us forward, and we want to hear more. So the speaker continues, "But with all the turmoil, poverty, and suffering that people in India have experienced, how can we share Gandhi's faith?" Quick! Tell us! We may not agree with you, but give us your opinion anyway. Now the speaker leads us right into the heart of the subject. Yes, there are terrible things in this world, but to a spiritual person they are like drops of oil in a vast ocean of good.

In our discussion of the opening moments of a talk, we should never forget that Dale Carnegie's overriding principle continues to apply: people's primary interest is always in themselves. So targeting the selfish interests of the audience is always one of the best ways to start. It's sure to get attention. That's only common sense—yet the use of this tactic is uncommon. For example, a speaker began a talk on the necessity of periodic physical exams. How did he open? He told the history of the medical organization with which he was affiliated. He described how it was organized and the service it was rendering. What a mistake! Listeners haven't the foggiest interest in how some organization was formed, but they are stupendously and eternally interested in themselves.

Why not recognize that fact and put it to use? Why not show how that health care organization is of vital concern to them? Try beginning with something like this: "Do you know how long you are expected to live according to the actuarial tables of the Social Security Administration? They have figured it all out. A man of thirty will probably live forty-four more years, and a woman of the same age will live fifty more. If the man survives to be sixty, he will probably have eighteen more years, and a woman will have twenty-three. Is that enough time to live? Will you be ready to let go at that point? No, no, we are all passionately eager for more life. Yet those tables are based upon millions of records. May you and I, then, somehow hope to beat them? Yes, with proper precaution, we may, but the very first step is to have a thorough physical examination."

Now, after you have dramatized why an examination is necessary, listeners might be interested in some organization formed to render that service. But to begin talking about the organization in an impersonal way is disastrous!

One more example. A student began a talk on the urgency of conserving our forests by saying, "We, as Americans, ought to be proud of our national resources." He then showed that we were wasting our timber at a shameless and indefensible pace. But the opening was too general and too vague. He did not make his subject seem vital to his audience. Suppose someone in the audience was in the printing business. The destruction of our forests would mean something very real to the cost of paper. Actually, the fate of the economy as a whole would be affected by the loss of millions of trees. So you could begin by saying, "The subject I am going to speak about affects your business, no matter what business that might be. It will, in some measure, affect the price of the food we eat and the rent that we pay. It touches the welfare and prosperity of us all, not only in this generation, but far into the future."

Is that exaggerating the importance of conserving our forests? No, I don't think it is. But it is certainly following Dale Carnegie's injunction to "paint the picture large and put the matter in a way that compels attention."

Don't be afraid to even shock your audience to some extent. Make them sit up and take notice. Say something that will jar them out of their daydreams. The bar has been set high today to get people's attention. To be an effective speaker you must command that attention by any means necessary. You've got to say something that is clear and hard-hitting, even if it invites controversy and disagreement. Read this opening for a talk on life in urban America:

"The American people are the worst criminals in the world. Cleveland has six times as many murders as London, and London is a much larger city. It has 170 times as many robberies, according to its population, as London has. More people are robbed in Cleveland every year, or assaulted with intent to rob, than in all of England, Scotland, and Wales combined. There are more murders in New York City than in all France or Germany or Italy or the British Isles."

This opening is successful because the speaker put power

and earnestness into his words. They lived. They breathed. But someone else might start a talk on the same subject with a bland list of statistics. The content might be flawless, but the spirit would be lacking.

Here's another example of an opening with real passion. The speaker starts out by admitting to feeling vulnerable, but then spins it in an entirely new direction:

"I have to admit that right now I feel like the proverbial deer in the headlights. Have you ever felt like that? I think you probably have, and I certainly hope so. Nobody would call it a pleasant feeling, but it's absolutely essential if you want to change and grow—not just in your work but in your life as a whole.

"Deer-in-the-headlights moments can be scary, painful, and sometimes even catastrophic, but they also hold the greatest opportunities for positive change and growth. I've been fortunate enough to meet a lot of successful people, and one thing they have in common is genuine appreciation for the most challenging moments of their careers.

"In fact, it's more than appreciation. Successful people feel actual *affection* for situations that pushed them to the edge. That makes perfect sense, because those deer-in-the-headlights moments are when you find out who you really are and what you can really do. And I promise this: you can do a lot more than you *think* you can, but unless you're different from almost everyone else on the planet, you have to find that out the hard way.

"Believe me, I know what extreme situations are like in business, and I know they're not a lot of fun in the moment. But I've have learned that when you're taken to the limit, the biggest danger is the temptation to give up, to freeze, to stand there watching the headlights approach until it's too late. That does happen to some people, or even to a lot of people. So we're going to explore not just how to prevent that from happening to you, but how you turn those extreme moments to your advantage—personally, professionally, and maybe even spiritually.

"What allows one person to handle pressure while others fold? What energy is missing from some people that, if present, would transform a dire circumstance into a priceless gift? By the end of this talk, you'll be able to answer those questions in great detail."

After hearing that opening, I think you would definitely pay attention to whatever comes next. I think you also understand by now that the arsenal of effective opening techniques has plenty of weapons. We've discussed some of the best ones, so in closing, let's briefly summarize what we've learned.

Once you're sure you have a rock-solid opening, make sure you feel relaxed when you first stand before the audience. You have every reason to feel relaxed. You've already got the most important part of your talk firmly in hand. So smile. Be confident and be in control. The floor is yours, and the audience will be on your side as soon as they hear your powerful opening. Remember, your best opportunity for impact is in the first seven seconds of your speech. So get to it.

Be aware of your body language. You yourself are the most powerful visual aid of all, so use motion and gesture for maximum effect. If the audience is not yet settled in and there's talking or shuffling of papers, just wait and look at the people involved. Say nothing—just look. You'll be amazed at the effect of this, and how quickly your authority increases.

Once you've completed your opening, pause briefly before going on. Make sure you're ready to go forward without any *um*s or *ah*s. Pausing is always fine as long as it's clearly intentional. Knowing that a pause now and then is perfectly admissible will help you concentrate on what you're saying next.

Keep control. No one will question your authority when you have the floor, provided you don't question it yourself. It will be smooth sailing from now on.

Make sure you have finished speaking before your audience has finished listening.

—Dorothy Sarnoff

Speak when you are angry—and you will make the best speech you'll ever regret.

—Laurence J. Peter

Every speaker has a mouth; an arrangement rather neat. Sometimes it's filled with wisdom. Sometimes it's filled with feet.

—Robert Orben

CHAPTER 8

The Power of Persuasion, Part One

In your career as a public speaker, you will sometimes encounter audiences that are resistant to your message. These audiences are not necessarily hostile—we'll deal with that possibility in a later chapter—but they are skeptical and questioning. They're like children who don't want to eat their dinner, despite that they're actually hungry. So, just as a parent turns the peas into a train going into the tunnel of the child's mouth, you have to find ways to persuade your listeners. You have to do it painlessly, so they don't even know they're being persuaded. They have to think they've reached your desired conclusion on their own. Instead of marveling at how smart you are, they have to congratulate themselves.

Generally speaking, there are three types of effective persuasion. Speakers can appeal to reason, they can appeal to emotion, or they can rely on the persuasive influence of their own character and personality. Let's begin this chapter by considering these one by one.

The Greek philosopher Aristotle, who wrote one of history's most complete studies of public speaking, expressed the wish that all communication could take place through reason. Many would probably agree with him. The French mathematician René Descartes, for example, chose to question everything—including his own existence. But he proved his existence, at least to his own satisfaction, by referring to his own thought process as evidence. If his being was in doubt, somebody had to be doing the doubting, and that somebody must have been Descartes himself. He expressed his conclusion through the famous axiom "I think, therefore I am." That's a completely logical statement. There's no emotion. There's no feeling about whether his being is a good thing or a bad thing. Pure rationality is linked to pure being, and the persuasiveness of the statement is linked to its transparent simplicity.

Aristotle might have been dismayed that emotional appeals also had advocates in the ancient world. The great Roman orator Cicero encouraged the use of emotion at the conclusion of a speech, but today emotional persuasion is used at virtually every opportunity. We might want to ask ourselves why the power of feeling is called upon so much more often than the power of mind—or maybe we might not want to ask ourselves that question. But this is definitely the way things are for modern public speakers.

Whether or not you agree with his viewpoint, former vice president Al Gore's film on global warming was a huge success. Besides winning an Academy Award for Best Documentary, it was seen by millions of people and made the topic of climate change into an urgent national issue. The movie is a film of a slide-show presentation that Al Gore had given more than a thousand times over the past several years. It combines statistics and scientific research with vivid images of glaciers and beaches. Without the emotional power of the images, the numbers and graphs could never have captured an audience. Al Gore had given the talk so many times that he knew how to give emotional power even to raw statistics. If you watch the film closely, you'll notice how often he presents his points in the form of questions. He'll ask, "What do you think the research showed?" or "Just how many years do you think this change is going to take?" Using this technique, even the projection of a simple bar graph can turn into a shocking revelation. Other speakers on all sides of the political landscape have gone ever further toward emotional appeals. Emotion is the most reliable way to connect with a large audience at the start of the twenty-first century. When you're a speaker, you simply must learn to master these techniques. When you're a listener, you should certainly learn to be aware of them as well.

A third avenue for a speaker is the persuasive appeal of his or her own character, and especially how this character is portrayed in the present talk. The traditional is that speakers need to appear knowledgeable about their topic, and benevolent as human beings. They have to seem smart and seem good for an audience to be persuaded.

Before you choose one or the other or even all of the above methods for effective persuasion, you need an effective framework through which to make your appeal. Even if you choose to be an extremely emotional speaker, you can't just get down on your knees and plead with people. You need a template in which your feelings and your ideas can be strongly presented, and through which your speech as a whole can take shape.

Please read this carefully, because in this chapter we'll be looking at the template you need to frame your message persuasively. Five aspects of your presentation must be at their best. They are the building blocks of persuasion, and every great speaker knows how to use them. The five building blocks are invention, arrangement, style, memory, and delivery. Let's look at them in order.

Invention is a word that we usually associate with creation, but it actually comes from a Latin root meaning "to find." Great speakers simply find the most effective vehicle for conveying their ideas. More often than not, this begins by understanding what is already in the mind of the audience, then connecting that knowledge with the message to be conveyed. Invention, therefore, refers to what a speaker says rather than how he or she says it.

In John F. Kennedy's inaugural address, for example, he wanted to sound a note of challenge for his listeners, but he also wanted to do this in a positive way. He wanted to move the nation out of the complacency that had characterized the 1950s and take it into a new era of social activism and responsibility. So how could this be accomplished? In his major speeches, Kennedy rarely used the "common man" approach. Presidents such as Lincoln and Truman had been hugely effective using the words and phrases of everyday life, but Kennedy had a different aura. He was a Harvard man but also a war hero. He was young for a president but had also seen the world. He was an intellectual but he had a sense of humor—not broad, backslapping humor, but a kind of dry wit. In terms of speaking, all this was invention—which doesn't mean it was false or insincere. It just means that this was the raw material that Kennedy had to work with. This was the personality that he had put into the minds of his readers. Now he had to find the words to convey his message in a way that was consistent with his public personality. He couldn't come out and burst into tears or make a joke about a traveling salesman. When people listened to Kennedy, it was as if they had tuned in to a certain frequency on a radio, and he had to stay within that frequency.

Read this famous passage from John F. Kennedy's inaugural speech:

"Let the word go forth from this time and place, to friend and foe alike, that the torch has been passed to a new generation of Americans—born in this century, tempered by war, disciplined by a hard and bitter peace, proud of our ancient heritage, and unwilling to witness or permit the slow undoing of those human rights to which this nation has always been committed, and to which we are committed today at home and around the world."

This could not credibly have been spoken by Dwight Eisenhower, Kennedy's predecessor, or by Harry Truman, or even by Abraham Lincoln. It couldn't even credibly have been spoken by John F. Kennedy himself except in his persona as leader of the nation—the persona that, in terms of public speaking, was a masterpiece of creativity. The first piece of the template is in place. We know who is speaking—not Jack Kennedy, not John Kennedy, not even John F. Kennedy. It's John Fitzgerald Kennedy, the president of the United States. Once we know the exact persona of the speaker, we're ready to determine exactly what that persona should say.

This leads us to arrangement, the next part of the template. *Arrangement* refers not to the specific words of a speech, but to the larger organization of the themes and ideas. Correct arrangement is extremely important. As a speaker, you don't want to convey the sense that you've gotten lost. You must make it clear to the audience that your talk has a beginning, a middle, and an end—that you know where you are, where you've been, and where you're going.

In the simplest kind of arrangement, this can be the old formula of "tell 'em what you're going to tell 'em, tell 'em, and then tell 'em what you told 'em." But in actual practice, a good speaker will employ a more subtle and persuasive arrangement. For example, you may begin by introducing an idea, then follow by introducing a contradictory idea, and finish with a third idea that resolves the contradiction. Depending on the time available, you can also employ a more or less formal introduction as well as a conclusion. You can add facts to support or refute the two ideas you've introduced. You can even digress into humor or stories from your own life. But whatever choices you make, they must seem to be intentional. They must convey a sense that you are in control of what you're saying, and when you say it. This is the essence of good arrangement.

Now we come to perhaps the most interesting element of the persuasiveness template—it's called *style*. If arrangement is the general order in which ideas are presented, style is the actual words by which they're expressed. Arrangement refers to *where* things will be said; style addresses *how* they'll be said. Over the years, more attention has been devoted to style than to any other aspect of oral presentation. This is where your identity as a speaker truly expresses itself. Through your style, people decide whether you're highly educated or a self-taught bumpkin. They learn whether you think the glass is half-full or half-empty. Based largely on your style, they decide whether they like you, and even more important, they decide whether they believe you.

To see how this happens, let's return again to John F. Kennedy's inaugural address. Try for a moment to put yourself in President Kennedy's place. You are becoming president after eight years of the Eisenhower administration. You are the youngest president ever, while Dwight Eisenhower was one of the oldest. Though in many respects he was a brilliant man—and certainly much more experienced as a statesman that John F. Kennedy—Eisenhower liked to avoid answering questions by seeming to bumble and mumble. Even a short sentence would have several *um*s and *ah*s. Often he appeared confused or distracted. This persona was an invention in terms of our template, but the country was largely tired of it. So if you were President Kennedy, how would you set yourself apart from your doddering predecessor? What style of expression would you use to emphatically put your mark on the presidency?

For many people today, a down-to-earth, "regular guy" style would be the first choice. We don't want to seem arrogant or pretentious, so we avoid elevated phrases or difficult vocabulary. This was certainly the style of another great twentieth-century communicator, President Ronald Reagan. He talked the way you might talk to your neighbor over the backyard fence when you were taking a break from mowing the lawn. But John F. Kennedy was different. He didn't want to be seen as a regular guy. He wanted to be able to quote Shakespeare and Churchill. He wanted to appeal to people's higher instincts and aspirations. So if that was the personal you had invented for yourself, how would you express it in words?

It's not an easy problem, is it? That's because few of us have chosen to embody the traits that made up John F. Kennedy. It wouldn't be right for us, but it was right for Kennedy, and he could bring it off. So he employed many stylistic flourishes in his inaugural address, some of which are still widely quoted today. He said, for example, "Ask not what your country can do for you; ask what you can do for your country."

Stylistically, you can see what a radical choice this represents. "Ask not" is such an artificial phrasing, not an everyday usage. But on that specific day, in that specific setting, it worked for John F. Kennedy. It was persuasive. It was perfect in terms of invention, arrangement, and style.

Now, by way of comparison, read this quote from a Ralph Nader speech announcing that he would run for president:

"I decided to seek your nomination because obstacles blocking solutions to our society's injustices and problems had to be overcome. Feelings of powerlessness and the withdrawal of massive numbers of Americans from both civic and political arenas are deeply troubling. This situation had to be addressed by a fresh political movement arising from the citizenry's labors and resources and dreams about what America could become at long last."

This is very different from Kennedy's style, and you would probably agree that it's much less effective. But the problem is not only with the style. The problem really comes from the first part of the template, from invention. Ralph Nader had invented himself as a speaker so that he had no choice but to talk this way. He couldn't talk like Kennedy any more than Kennedy could have talked like him. Nader had not laid the foundation for a powerful public-speaking personality. He was stuck with being a public-policy wonk and he sounded like one, but at least it was consistent with who he was. It was his authentic self.

As a speaker, you should choose the style you employ at a particular event just as carefully as you choose what you wear. If you're addressing a group of farmers at a livestock auction, you wouldn't dress the way you might for a formal wedding or state dinner. By the same token, you wouldn't try to persuade those farmers of anything using the same phrases you might use with the queen of England. The key is to understand your intentions and needs in a particular setting. Then you can speak in a way that fulfills those intentions and needs—provided that it is also congruent with your personality. Your speech has to sound right for who you are. For you to be persuasive, your invention and style must be consistent.

In chapter 1, we spoke about the danger of trying to memorize a presentation word for word. Memorization can work, unless it doesn't. Because if you've memorized a speech and your memory suddenly deserts you in front of the audience, you're pretty much stuck. However, the next element of our persuasion template is actually called *memory*, but we need to understand exactly what that word means in a modern context.

At one time, memory was considered the truest indicator of intelligence. Today we tend to think of geniuses in terms of aptitude for math or science, but in the past memory defined superior intelligence. Possibly because of this expectation, plenty of people displayed amazing memories. Even average men and women, often without much education, could recite passages from the Bible that were thousands of words long. Some public speakers could deliver memorized speeches that went on for hours. It was expected of an intelligent person, and good speakers wanted to fulfill that expectation. Consider Theodore Roosevelt, for example. One day in Wisconsin he delivered a ninety-minute speech that he had written himself—a remarkable achievement, especially since he had been shot just before he started talking. Fortunately, the manuscript of his speech was in his pocket and slowed down the bullet enough to keep him from being killed. The downside was, he had to deliver the speech from memory, which he did—and then he went to the hospital.

But that was then, and this is now. Few people today could deliver a long, completely memorized speech, and there's no expectation that they should do so. But memory still plays a big role in persuasive public speaking. Here, for example, is a speaking technique that gets a lot of people into trouble. You've probably seen it used, and maybe you've even used it yourself. You complete the introduction of your talk, then say, "There are five important points I want to make about this issue." Some people even make it harder on themselves. They'll say, "I have seven points," or even nine points.

So what happens? They get through the first three points, then they start wondering a little bit. After a few more points, they're really wondering. How many have I done? How many do I have left to go? And if you look around during a speech like that, you can also see some members of the audience counting on their fingers.

Lots of other things that can happen along these lines. Sometimes speakers will refer to a quote that perfectly illustrates the point they're making—and then can't remember the quote. Sometimes they'll mention an idea they want to elaborate on later in the talk—but then they never do.

This is where memory, or failure of memory, comes into play. You could also call it poise, or concentration. When you've mastered this aspect of the persuasion template, you don't get yourself into those kinds of fixes. If you say you're going to cover seven points, you cover seven points—and believe me, your listeners will be impressed when that happens. If you have a certain organization for your talk in mind, you're able to manifest that organization in the talk itself. You never get confused or befuddled. Or almost never.

I say almost never because sooner or later every speaker hits a bump in the road, but this too can be dealt with through the power of memory. In classical times, when orators were expected to know long speeches by heart, it was understood that even the best memory would fail from time to time. To prepare for that, every speaker had some fallback material that could be deployed as soon as there was a problem. It might be a favorite story or a powerful quotation, kept continually ready and practiced, just as schoolchildren practice a fire drill. If a speaker starts to draw a blank, the ability to shift smoothly into backup content is an important aspect of professionalism. You always want to be prepared for this. You should never seem to be "at a loss for words."

As we're discussing these things, you might be thinking, "Can't a lot of these problems be avoided by using a PowerPoint presentation? Can't we just take the pressure off ourselves by projecting what we're supposed to say up on a screen?"

That's an important question, and I'll address it before the close of the chapter. Please see if I remember to do what I said!

But first we need to look at the final aspect of the persuasion template. So far we've covered invention, arrangement, style, and memory. The concluding element is *delivery*. We discussed this concept in chapter 1, but it's so important that we need to revisit it now. Style, you'll recall, is the way things are said, and by that I mean the choice of words and sentence constructions. Style can express itself on the printed page just as well as in oral presentation. Delivery, however, is not just what is said, but how it is said. For this reason, delivery is exclusively a feature of spoken presentation.

To be persuasive, you should be absolutely certain that the manner in which you say things is the way you want them to be heard. Practice your delivery as much as you can, and practice in every way possible. Practice with your friends and family, and, if possible, practice with some people you don't know well. Practice talking in front of a mirror. Make audio and video recordings of your presentation. Try different ways of saying the same sentence and see which one works best. You yourself must be persuaded that you have the best possible delivery before you can hope to persuade anyone else. All it takes is practice.

Every speech is an invention, or at least it should be. What worked before can't be counted on to work again, because no two oral presentations are the same. The locations are probably different, the audiences are almost certainly not the same, and even if everything else is as close to the same as it could possibly be, the moment of time for each speech is always new. So you'll need to come up with something that solves the specific challenges you're facing in a specific setting. You need to be creative. More than that, you need to be inventive.

What are some of the best techniques for stimulating your inventive faculties to solve problems, make decisions, and achieve goals? The strategies needed to put together a good speech are not so different from what would facilitate any other type of invention. So let's look at some of those strategies right now.

Think combination. Everything you see, hear, touch, taste, and smell during the day offers you the opportunity to consider new combinations of ideas. When you brush your teeth, you might think of a toothbrush that contains the toothpaste in the handle. You might combine your mirror with a motto reminding you to start the day right. It might read, "How can I increase my service today?" or "Have no small dreams!" That's thinking combination. A simple pencil is a combination of wood, carbon, rubber, paint, and metal. People have come up with great concepts that have led to profits, patents, and even billion-dollar companies by finding new combinations.

You can do the same thing with ideas, or even with words. An effective speech should be original not only in what is said, but in the *way* it's said. When you have an idea you want to get across, challenge yourself to accomplish that in the most original way possible. How can you link your idea to another one in a combination that will be memorable and inspiring to your listeners? What forms of expression can you use to not only say something new and different, but also to say it in a new and different way?

Think adaptation. In 1948, a Swiss engineer named George de Mestral returned from a walk through a field of weeds and found some burrs clinging to his cloth jacket. Studying one of the burrs under a microscope, he saw a maze of thin strands with tiny hooks at the ends. These hooks could cling to fabrics or animal fur. De Mestral immediately recognized the potential for a practical new fastener, although it took eight years to develop and perfect the invention. Today Velcro is a well-known, extremely useful product. It makes all kinds of other products better, from shoes to boxing gloves.

Whenever something catches your eye, explore ways you might be able to use it in your public speaking. You can and should do this regardless of the original context. Do you know how braille was invented? Have you ever heard how chewing gum came into being? Look it up! These interesting stories can add important and memorable content to your talks. It's just a matter of adapting from the original context to the purposes of a specific presentation and audience.

Think substitution. When you study powerful speeches from the past—including the ones in this book—think of ways you can use some of the same techniques while substituting specifics to meet the needs of your audience. For example, before a decisive battle against the ancient Persian empire, Alexander the Great spoke to his soldiers about the courage of their fathers and grandfathers in previous battles. This built up the confidence of Alexander's troops. They saw that they'd come from a legacy of "winners" against great odds, and they believed that they could be winners too.

It's easy to see how this same concept can be useful in addressing a sales meeting, or a sports team, or even a high school student preparing for an exam. There are no patents on public-speaking strategies, so take full advantage of them. Learn from the greats, and substitute from their tactics to fulfill your needs.

Think big. Why do you think there are now dozens of players in the National Football League who weigh more than three hundred pounds? It isn't because men that size are better athletes than the players of the past, or more effective blockers and tacklers. To a large extent, this change has come about because audiences want to see *gigantic* human beings in physical combat. It's the same reason spectators in the Roman Colosseum wanted to see elephants. Something about bigness is inherently exciting to human beings.

Here's a hint for putting this principle to work. Find ways of mentioning large numbers in your speeches. It doesn't much matter what point you're trying to make as long as words such as *million* and *billion* come out of your mouth. Be sure to pronounce those words with as much enthusiasm as you possibly can. You'll be amazed at the energizing effect this can have on an audience.

The late astronomer and bestselling author Carl Sagan was a master at this. His topic, which was the universe, allowed him to say *million, billion,* and even *trillion* as often as he wanted. It was one of the things that made him an effective speaker. Sagan's audiences probably never realized what he was doing, but the big numbers were an effective rhetorical device. Think big, and talk big. Your listeners will be happy to follow your lead.

As a speaker, you should always be rearranging things, changing pace, altering sequences, or even starting over from scratch. If you want to spur your listeners to action, fill your talks with combinations, adaptations, inventions—and always think big! This kind of presentation increases the scope of your speeches and enables you to achieve fuller use of your energies. So when you're preparing a speech, let your mind work for you. Take nothing for granted. What can be changed and improved and articulated in new ways?

We've now reached the end of chapter 8, but before concluding I want to discuss PowerPoint presentations. These have become a fixture of speeches, and no book of this nature would be complete without talking about them.

It might seem that PowerPoint technology can instantly turn anyone into a polished speaker. You don't have to worry about having a well-organized talk because it's all projected up on the wall for you. You only have to read it and make some comments. But if that's all speakers *have* to do, that's all that most are *going* to do. All too easily, the PowerPoint becomes a replacement for the presenter. Instead of the technology being a visual aid for the speakers, the speakers become an audio aid for the machine. This strips presentations of their most powerful element, which is, or ought to be, the presence of the speakers themselves.

The Greeks had a word for this, *ethos*, which referred to the personal appeal of the speaker. Ethos reflected both the verbal and the nonverbal elements of a speech. These had to be carefully managed and orchestrated for a presentation to succeed. With PowerPoint, however, many of the elements that establish ethos are erased. Speakers don't look at the audience and the audience doesn't look at the speakers. Nonverbal cues, such as eye contact, are lost. Presentations tend to be read off the slides or from handouts, which flattens delivery. The whole event suffers a general "dumbing down."

That effect is the main drawback of PowerPoint, but there are also some technical issues. For example, PowerPoint works better with images than it does with text. PowerPoint text generally allows less than ten lines of text on a slide, and no more than six words per line. So if you try to cover a significant amount of text in a presentation, you have to move through a lot of slides. That means a lot of clicks and a lot of jerky movements, which detracts from the presentation. But speakers can get to the point where they just say, "Who cares?" It's so easy to rely on the slides they just do not worry about it.

This is unfortunate because almost all business presentations given with PowerPoint would be better without it. This would involve a little more effort and a little more study, but that's what this book is for. If speakers aren't willing to make that effort, that means they don't want to take a little time to master critical skills.

That you're reading this right now proves that you want to fulfill your potential as a public speaker. So put aside the PowerPoint and read this chapter again. Master the template of invention, arrangement, style, memory, and delivery. Then go on to chapter 9 where you'll learn even more about persuasion.

It's quite simple. Say what you have to say and when you come to a sentence with a grammatical ending, sit down.

—Winston Churchill

Speech is power: speech is to persuade, to convert, to compel.

—Ralph Waldo Emerson

The right word may be effective, but no word was ever as effective as a rightly timed pause.

—Mark Twain

CHAPTER 9

The Power of Persuasion, Part Two

The human mind works in fascinating and even mysterious ways. It's not easy to make a statement about the mind that is universally true, but here's one that comes close: "Every idea, concept, or conclusion which enters the mind will be completely believed unless hindered by some conflicting idea." Do you see what this means? If we present people with an idea, it isn't necessary to convince them of the idea's truth as long as we prevent conflicting ideas from arising. So if you read a sentence like "Acme hubcaps are the best hubcaps on the market," you will believe that to be true unless you have contradictory information. And if no contradictory information is forthcoming, you will continue to believe it indefinitely.

All living creatures are supplied at birth with everything they need for survival. All creatures except one are supplied with a set of instincts that will do the job for them. Most creatures don't need much of a brain. Human beings, however, need not only a brain but also a *mind*. In Archibald MacLeish's play *The Secret of Freedom* a character says, "The only thing about a man that is man is his mind. Everything else you can find in a pig or a horse." That's uncomfortably true.

Consider a magnificent eagle. To see one of them swooping

down to pluck a fish from the water on a single pass is astonishing. More astonishing still is the eagle's eyesight. Because of its need to see small rodents moving in the grass from high altitudes or a fish just inches under the surface of the water, the eagle's eyes take up just about all the space in its head. For the eagle, its eyes are the most important thing, and everything else works in unison with them. Its brain is tiny and rudimentary. It doesn't think or plan or remember. It simply acts in accordance with stimuli.

That's the way it is for most living creatures. Only one takes twenty years to mature and has dominion over all the rest—and has today the power to destroy all life on earth in a couple of hours. Only one is given the godlike power to fashion its own life according to the images it holds in its mind.

The human mind is the one thing that separates us from the rest of the creatures on earth. Everything that means *anything* to us comes to us through our minds: our love of our families, our beliefs, our talents, our knowledge, and all of our abilities. Everything is reflected through our minds. Anything that comes to us in the future will almost certainly come to us as a result of the use of our minds.

Yet, the mind is the last place on earth the average person will turn to for help. Why? Why don't people automatically turn on their own vast mental resources when faced with a problem? It's because they never learned how to think. Most people go to great lengths to avoid thinking when they're faced with a problem. They will ask advice from people who don't usually know any more than they do: next-door neighbors, members of their families, and friends stuck in the same mental traps that they are. Few of them use the power of their mind to overcome obstacles.

Yet all aspects of successful living, including becoming an effective public speaker, are a matter of solving the problems that stand between where we are now and the point we wish to reach. No one is without problems. They're part of living. But we waste so much time worrying about the *wrong* problems! A reliable estimate of the things people worry shows the following:

Things that will never happen: 40%

Things in the past that can never be changed: 30%

Needless worries about health: 12%

Petty miscellaneous worries: 10%

Legitimate worries: 8%

In short, 92 percent of the average person's worries take up valuable time, cause painful stress, even mental anguish, yet are absolutely unnecessary. The legitimate worries are of two kinds: the problems we can solve, and the problems beyond our ability to personally solve. Most of our real problems fall into the first group, the ones we can solve if we'll just learn how.

The average working person has at his or her disposal an enormous amount of free time. If we sleep eight hours every night during the year, we still have about six thousand waking hours, of which less than two thousand would be spent in a forty-hour-per-week job. This leaves four thousand hours a year when a person is neither working nor sleeping. In these "discretionary hours" a person can do pretty much as he or she pleases.

Suppose you take just one hour a day, five days a week, and devote this hour to exercising your development as a public speaker. You don't even have to do it on weekends. Pick one hour a day and set it aside for the same purpose that you're reading this book: to make yourself the best speaker you can possibly be.

During this daily hour, sit down with a blank sheet of paper and a pencil. At the top of the page write your most immediate goal for your public speaking career. It might be overcoming fear or acquiring more speaking engagements. There are dozens of possibilities. Then, since your future depends on the way you achieve your goals, write down as many ideas as you can for attaining this objective. Try to think of at least twenty possibilities. You won't always get twenty, but even a single idea can be valuable.

There are two important points to remember. First, consistently devoting an hour to this is not always easy. Second, most of your ideas won't be especially good. This exercise is like starting any new habit. At first your mind will be a little reluctant to be "hauled out of bed." But as you think about your work and ways in which it might be improved, write down every idea that pops into your head, no matter how absurd it might seem.

The most important thing that this hour accomplishes is to deeply embed your goal into your subconscious mind and start the whole vital machine reworking the first thing every morning. Twenty ideas a day, if you can come up with that many, total one hundred a week, even skipping weekends.

An hour a day, five days a week, totals 260 hours a year and still leaves you 3,740 hours of leisure time. This means you'll be thinking about public speaking and ways of improving your performance for six and a half forty-hour workweeks! And you'll still have seven hours a day to do as you please.

When you start each day by thinking about speaking, you'll find that your mind will continue to work all day long. At odd moments, when you least expect it, great ideas will begin to bubble up from your subconscious. When they do, write them down as soon as you can. Just one great idea can completely revolutionize your work and, as a result, your life.

Each of us tends to underestimate our own abilities. We should realize that we have within ourselves deep reservoirs of great ability, even genius, that can be tapped if we'll just dig deep enough. It's the miracle of your mind. When you write your goal at the top of that sheet of paper, don't worry or become concerned about it. Think of it as only waiting to be reached, a problem only waiting to be solved. Face it with faith and bend all the great powers of your mind toward solving it. And you *will* solve it!

These observations about the relationship between the mind and public speaking are especially pertinent to persuasion. We like to think of ourselves as logical, thinking beings, but logic does not come into play until certain conditions are met. Before we can compare one idea to another, we need to have at least two ideas. Until then, persuasion is the result of suggestion or instinct rather than logical processes. If I say to you, "Cell phones are completely harmless," and no contradictory evidence is on your mental landscape, you can be persuaded simply by the suggestion I have made. But if someone has shown you an Internet website that raises questions about the safety of cell phones, then I will have to show you evidence to prove my assertion. I will have to convince you by logical argument rather than by suggestion alone.

This has important implications for public speaking, in which information reaches a listener quickly with no opportunity to review it. The most persuasive speakers rely much more on suggestion than on argument. For the most part, listeners actually appreciate this. After all, it's easy to believe; doubting is more difficult. Experience and knowledge and thinking are necessary before we can doubt and ask questions intelligently. Tell a child that Santa Claus comes down the chimney, and the child will accept this until further knowledge causes change.

Your strategy in persuading people should first and foremost be to put an idea firmly in their minds, and second to keep contradictory and opposing ideas from arising. If you become skilled in reaching those goals, you will have both success and profit in public speaking. It's that simple.

So how can you make this happen? First, be aware that opposing ideas are much less likely to arise when the main idea is presented with feeling and contagious enthusiasm. I say *contagious* because enthusiasm is just that. It quiets critical impulses. It's a natural barrier to all dissenting, negative, and opposing ideas. When your aim is persuasiveness, remember that it's more productive to stir emotions than to arouse thoughts. Feelings are more powerful than cold ideas. But to generate feelings, you need sincerity and earnestness and enthusiasm. Insincerity will ruin even the best delivery. Regardless of the pretty phrases you may concoct; regardless of the illustrations you may assemble; regardless of the harmony of your voice and the grace of your gestures—if you aren't sincere, it's all a waste. So if you want to persuade an audience, first persuade yourself. Once that's done, you can speak to the audience with sincerity. Let that sincerity resonate in your voice and shine in your eyes from the moment you stand up in front of your listeners until the moment you sit down.

Sincerity needs to be combined with intensity. Along with your authenticity, you need to communicate your energy. Three useful tactics for doing that are *repetition, association,* and *contrast.* If it might seem that these terms are self-explanatory, but let's look a bit closer. Probably more is going on here than you think.

When a new product is introduced into the marketplace, people don't buy it just because it suddenly appears on the shelves. Research shows that consumers need at least nine exposures to a product—whether on billboards or in TV spots or in print ads—before they even notice that the product exists. Once they do notice, several things happen. First, the name and the visual image of the product are remembered, and the memory becomes reinforced as more exposures occur.

The exact same thing happens in an oral presentation. The first time you introduce an idea—especially if it's not phrased in some catchy way—it will probably go right by your listeners. In one ear and out the other, as the saying goes. But if you keep saying it, and if you do so in a novel or interesting way, people will not only remember it, they'll also begin to anticipate it. But that's not all. The amazing thing is, they'll also begin to accept it as true. In a strange fact of human nature, repetition has persuasive power. Simply by presenting the same information several times, you can increase the intensity and the persuasiveness of your message.

"It is not by advancing a truth once or twice, or even ten

times, that the people will adopt it," said Franklin Roosevelt. "Incessant repetition is required to impress political truths upon the public mind. By always hearing the same facts, people gradually give them a place in the corner of their minds. Soon they would no more think of doubting it than they would doubt their religious or patriotic beliefs."

An earlier president, Woodrow Wilson, made the same point in a different way. Once, as a boy, Wilson asked his mother why she had repeated the same fact to him twenty times. She replied, "Because you haven't learned it after nineteen."

One word of caution about using the tool of repetition: unless you have a novel way of saying the same thing over and over, your repetition could become tedious. If your point can be made in just a few words, you might want to create a simple rhyme. Recall Johnnie Cochran's couplet about O. J. Simpson's glove: "If it doesn't fit, you must acquit." You can also repeat a single idea in more expanded forms, provided you have the vocabulary to do this in a graceful and interesting manner. From your vantage point behind the podium you'll be able to tell if this is working. If a number of people seem to be looking at their watches, it's not working!

Association is a further development of repetition, and the two need to be used in tandem. For example, we mentioned in an earlier chapter that telling stories about air travel usually catches the interest of an audience. Being on an airplane is the kind of experience that they're familiar with and can relate to, but it's still enough of a novelty for most people that they're interested in it. Let's imagine that you want to make a point about the importance of exercise. One way is to just present some statistics or to reference some book or article you've read.

That might work, but if you want to hugely increase the impact of what you're saying, simply mention that you read the article while you were on an airplane. It's almost like magic, but it's true. Just associating your message with certain settings and experiences has a major amplifying effect. It's so easy. You haven't changed anything about the content of what you're saying, but it's dramatically more persuasive.

Or consider this use of association. A classic argument in the history of religion is known as the blind watchmaker. Here's how it goes. An atheist once declared to a devout clergyman that there was no God and challenged the clergyman to disprove his contention. The clergyman quietly took out his pocket watch, opened the case, and showed the works to the unbeliever, saying, "If I were to tell you that those levers and wheels and springs were put together by a sightless person, would you believe me? Would you believe that a blind man, operating by trial and error, could assemble a watch? Wouldn't you question my intelligence if I made such a statement? Of course, you would. But look up at the stars. Every one of them has its perfect appointed course and motion—the earth and planets around the sun, and the whole group pitching along at more than a million miles a day. Each star is another sun with its own group of worlds, rushing on through space like our own solar system. Yet there are no collisions, no disturbance, and no confusion. All quiet, efficient, and controlled. Is it easier to believe that they just happened, or that someone made them like that?"

You don't have to be a believer in the theory of intelligent design—or in evolution, for that matter—to see that this is an impressive argument from a rhetorical perspective. What technique did the speaker use? Well, he began by establishing a common ground—an association. He got his opponent agreeing with him about the watch, and that led the way to the next step. Then he went on to show that belief in a deity is as simple, as inevitable, as belief in a sighted watchmaker rather than a blind one.

But suppose the clergyman had taken a much more aggressive approach. Suppose he'd said, "Don't be stupid! You don't know what you are talking about!" What would have happened? There would probably have been an argument—perhaps fiery, but almost certainly futile. The atheist would have defended his opinion just as fanatically as the clergyman attacked it. Why? Because it was his opinion, and his precious, indispensable self-esteem would have been threatened. His pride would have been at stake.

Since pride is such a fundamentally explosive characteristic of human nature, it's much better to get people's pride working for you instead of against you. To do this, you need to show that the thing you propose is similar to something that your listeners already believe. That makes it easier for the listeners to accept than reject your proposal. It prevents contradictory and opposing ideas from arising to block what you've said.

The clergyman we've mentioned showed clear appreciation of how the human mind functions. Most people lack this subtle ability to unite with a listener's beliefs. Most people imagine that to win a war, they need to use a frontal attack. But in that kind of confrontation there is usually no winner. A lot of damage can be done, but neither side has persuaded the other of anything.

Regarding association, our concerns about any topic can

change from one situation to another. For example, one audience may be focused on the financial side of a question, while another may want to know about environmental impact. We can refer to these differences as matters of prominence. Listeners vary in the prominence they assign to various issues. For maximum effect, you'll want to associate your arguments with ideas that you know to be prominent in your listeners' minds. That knowledge is crucially important and will fundamentally influence the strategies you employ. When an issue is prominent to a group of listeners, they are likely to be well-informed and skeptical of radical change. With such an audience, you'll need strong, well-thought-out reasons to achieve persuasion. You may not need a lot of reasons, but the ones you invoke had better be good. In contrast, an audience that does not see your issue as especially prominent is likely to be more accepting of what you say. Instead of wanting to hear only your strongest arguments, they'll be willing to hear pretty much everything. So you can use the tool of association freely.

Our third tool is contrast, and this is probably the most powerful of all. As with repetition and association, the power of contrast connects to a fundamental trait of human nature. People are much sharper in recognizing *differences* between things rather than noticing the inherent qualities of something on its own. People are comfortable making judgments about things, but like to make them in contrast to something else. So when they say someone is smart or talkative, they actually mean the person is smarter or more talkative than other people.

This human tendency is true not only for arguments and ideas, but on the level of physical sensation as well. Put your left hand in a bowl of cold water and your right in water that's warmer. Leave them there for a while, then plunge both together into a bowl of lukewarm water. The left hand will feel hot while the right will feel cold. It's a hardwired principle of contrast. Put light next to dark and it seems lighter. A stale smell will seem worse after a sweet smell. Many more examples come from all areas of life.

Here's an example of how the principle of contrast works. Imagine you're a research-and-development executive in a large home-products corporation. Your company is trying to decide whether to build a new lab for your division. You've been assigned to investigate the costs of building the lab. You've been given some budgetary guidelines, but the amount that the company is willing to spend hasn't yet been finalized.

You'd like to have the best lab possible for your R & D work, so when you present your research to a meeting of senior executives, you wisely decide to use the principles we've been discussing. You're sincere and you're enthusiastic. You use repetition and association. You make especially good use of contrast. Here's how.

"Ladies and gentlemen," you say, "I'm very aware of the amount of money that's available for this project, and I want to present a couple of options in the clearest possible way. For example, the minimum expenditure to build a new lab would be three million dollars. Let me show you what a three-million-dollar lab would look like."

You show a graphic—it can be an architect's rendering of the exterior or a floor plan—of a rather unimpressive structure. It shouldn't be over-the-top bad, but rudimentary. It should be a plain-vanilla R & D lab. Or maybe vanilla that's been left out of the freezer about ten minutes too long.

If you do this correctly, you will create a sense of moderate to severe disappointment in your listeners. It will be unspoken, it may even be unconscious, but it will be there. Now you're ready to project a new graphic, this time reflecting a higher budget and a significantly more attractive result.

The degree of persuasion you'll achieve by showing the two graphics will be much, much higher than if you'd shown the second one alone. Contrast is so simple, but so powerful. Don't overthink this power, just let it work for you.

We should also look at a couple of variations of contrast. Sometimes you may want to present an extreme contrast instead of two ideas that are more or less in the same ballpark. If a speaker wanted to address climate change, he or she might portray a truly dire scenario compared with a much better one. The audience would be called on to choose between a total environmental mess and a much more livable situation. This all-or-nothing contrast might be a good choice when you're trying to get people to make major lifestyle decisions.

Here's another alternative. Instead of presenting just two choices, you can go in the opposite direction and offer as many as possible. You can say, "Here's what we get if we spend one million, or two million, or three million," and so forth. When you take that approach, two possibilities arise. First, the listeners might try to simplify the decision. They'll try to break it down to a choice between two options—and the clearer the contrast, the better. Or they might be so confused that they're unable to make any decision at all. So if you're in a presentation in which your real goal is to buy time, offering lots of contrasting choices can be effective. There's a good chance the matter will be sent back to the drawing board for further study. You've really persuaded your audience not to be persuaded for the time being.

So far in this chapter we've looked at a few of the most powerful tools a speaker can employ for persuasion. We've seen how sincerity, repetition, association, and especially contrast can help you achieve your goals. There's so much more to say about persuasion, however, that for the balance of this chapter we're going to pick up the pace a bit. We've discussed the major axioms of persuasion in detail; now we're going to look at as many secondary principles as we can. These quick, hard-hitting tactics can immediately get readers on your side. You may not be able to use all of them in a single presentation, but you should definitely use as many as possible.

For example, people are interested in *activity*. Their attention is drawn to things that move, flash, or blink. If it's at all appropriate, use a prop of that kind in your talk, especially when you need to perk up the attention of your listeners. But when you're not using it, get it out of their sight. If you refer to a map of the United States, make sure the states are brightly colored and that the whole map can easily be seen from anywhere in the room. But when you're finished with it, take it down or shut off the projector. Don't let the object that worked so well as a novelty become a distraction for the same reasons.

Second, tangible, vivid words and images are more persuasive than hypotheticals or abstractions. So use as many proper nouns, place names, and brand names as you can. Compare these two sentences: "When I moved to a new town, I had to drive around to find the supermarket" and "When I moved to Phoenix, I spent a lot of time in my Honda looking for the

Food Giant." By making readers present in the picture you've painted, you persuade them that the picture is real.

Just as it's important to create presence, *proximity* is also essential. People pay more attention to things that are close to them than to things that are far away. So as soon as you've got enough experience to do it comfortably, don't be afraid to come out from behind the podium and interact with the audience a little. You should also build proximity into what you say as well as where you are. If you're looking for ways to illustrate a point, think of a news story that got your attention that morning. Refer to places and events and people that are recent, immediate, or nearby. Can you say something interesting or positive about the previous speaker? Can you mention someone in the audience by name—especially someone who's known to the other audience members?

Listeners like things that are familiar and pay attention to things that are new and different. You can put both those tendencies to work by saying something new about a person, place, or thing that they already know about. It's even better if they're certain that they already know everything about that particular topic. Who was the person who introduced you? What interesting fact were you able to find out about that person as you prepared for this event? How can you build that fact into your talk in a way that will help the audience warm to you? The more you can foster warmth, the more you can build trust—and the more trust you build, the more persuasive you will be.

Suspense is another great attention-getting tool, and when you pay it off correctly, it can make your message persuasive. In public speaking, building suspense doesn't mean making people worried or frightened. It's just sharing information in an interesting and somewhat surprising way. For example, as the next presidential election approaches, you can ask a suspense-building question about politics. Something like, since 1960, how many senators have run for president, and how many senators have won? You don't have to give the answer right away. You probably shouldn't. Just say, "I'll share that information with you in a moment, and I think the numbers will surprise you." In case you find this unbearably suspenseful, at the time of this writing forty senators have run for president since 1960, and the only sitting senators to attain the presidency were John F. Kennedy and Barack Obama.

One caveat about using suspense is to make sure that the information you finally reveal is important enough to warrant the interest you've created. Audiences become irritated when a speaker says something like "More about that later"—then says little of value or forgets about the point altogether. A good way to prepare for this is to run your material by some friends. If their reaction seems weak or forced when they hear the payoff, don't use it in your speech.

Conflict is probably even more reliable than suspense for capturing listener's interest. People pay attention to a good fight, especially when the issue seems clear and demanding of action. When he addressed a joint session of Congress on September 20, 2001, President George W. Bush said, "Freedom and fear are at war. The advance of human freedom, the great achievement of our time and the great hope of every time, now depends on us." Most commentators consider this the best speech of the Bush presidency. At this dramatic moment in American history, the president described it as a clear conflict between good and evil. You may never have to address the nation after an attack that killed three thousand people, but bear in mind that listeners want to be challenged and mobilized. Persuade them that they're in the right, and the rest will come easily.

No matter how many persuasion techniques you use, it's absolutely essential to use them in a clear and organized context. Because individual members of your audience will vary in their response to your techniques, you should always use a variety of persuasive tools. But while the positive reactions of listeners will differ, you will get a universally negative reaction if your talk seems scattered and unfocused. Ideas that are logically related and consistent give listeners confidence in you as a speaker. The more an audience can follow the links of your thinking, the easier it will be for them to maintain their overall attention to your message. A disjointed, random collection of thoughts makes an audience start thinking about almost anything except what you're trying to tell them.

Studies suggest that people are more attentive when they know what to look for. Cuing the audience—that is, preparing them for what to expect—can be done in two ways. In the first method, known as forecasting, you simply tell the audience what the major divisions of the speech will be. Say something like "First, I'll review the two primary reasons for the growth in population west of the Rockies, then I'll discuss the implications of that growth for the building-supply industry." When used as part of your introduction, forecasting gives the audience an overview of the entire speech and allows them to anticipate major divisions.

A second means of conveying strong organization comes during transitions between sections of your speech. Transitions can act as verbal signposts, indicating the next major point that's to come. Transitions can be phrased in many ways, and the ability to handle them gracefully is a real test of a high impact speaker. It's good if you can be clever, but if nothing occurs to you, just try to be clear. Use a serviceable transition like "With this brief history as a basis, we can consider the next step" or "Here's the second of my three alternatives." Transitions cause problems for many speakers, but they're really easy if you keep their true purpose in mind.

There are three things to aim at in public speaking: first, to get into your subject, then to get your subject into yourself, and lastly, to get your subject into the heart of your audience.

—Alexander Gregg

Be still when you have nothing to say; when genuine passion moves you, say what you've got to say, and say it hot.

—D. H. Lawrence

Grasp the subject, the words will follow.

—Cato the Elder

CHAPTER 10

Creativity and the Magic Formula

All creative people are unique, but they all share certain broadly defined qualities. In any field, for example, and certainly in public speaking, creative men and women realize that the human mind is an inexhaustible storehouse. But to draw from this storehouse, we must constantly expand its stock of information, thoughts, and wisdom. We must reach out for ideas from every possible source, including the ideas of others, while always giving them credit for their contributions. Everyone has ideas; they're free, and many of them are excellent. By first listening to the ideas of others and thinking them through before judging them, creative people avoid prejudice and closed-mindedness. This is the way to maintain a climate of invention that's conducive to growth.

Ideas are like slippery fish. They seem to have a peculiar knack of getting away from us. Because of this, creative people always keep a pad and a pencil handy. This is simply a must-have. When you get an idea, write it down. You could even type it into your phone or send yourself an e-mail. Many people have found their whole lives changed by a single great thought. By capturing ideas immediately, you don't risk forgetting them.

Widening your circle of friends and broadening your base of knowledge are two more effective techniques of the creative person. Having a sincere interest in others, creative people listen carefully when someone else is talking. They're intensely observant, absorbing everything seen and heard. They behave as if everyone they meet wears a sign that reads, "My ideas and interest may offer the hidden key to your next success." So they make it a point to always talk with other people's interest in mind. This pays off in a flood of new ideas and information that would otherwise be lost forever.

Creative people anticipate achievement. They expect to succeed, and the remarkable productivity engendered by this attitude affects everyone around them. It makes *others* more creative.

Problems are challenges to creative minds. Without problems, there would be little reason to think at all. Creative individuals know it's a waste of time merely to worry about problems, so they wisely invest that same time and energy in solving problems.

When creative people get an idea, they take a series of steps designed to improve it. They think it through in new directions. They build big ideas from small ones and new ideas from old ones. They associate ideas, combine them, adapt them, substitute them, magnify them, rearrange them, and even reverse them.

Creative and productive people are not creative and productive for the material outcome. They're simply driven by the need to be creative and productive. They'd be that way even if they lived on a deserted island with no one benefiting from or even aware of what they were doing. They experience the joy of producing something. Material benefit to themselves or others is welcome, but only secondary.

Every creative person is an artist in the truest and widest sense of the word—and artists are often misunderstood. A group of artists who were rejected by the establishment of their time formed their own association in self-defense. They were Degas, Pissaro, Monet, Cézanne, and Renoir. Five of the greatest artists of all time, all doing what they believed in, in the face of total rejection.

Renoir was laughed at and rejected not only by the public but by his fellow artists, yet he went right on painting. Even Manet said to Monet, "Renoir has no talent at all. You who are his friend should tell him kindly to give up painting."

Renoir, in his later life, suffered terribly from rheumatism, especially in his hands. He lived in constant pain. When Matisse visited the aging painter, he saw that every stroke was causing renewed pain. Matisse asked, "Why do you still have to work? Why continue to torture yourself?" Renoir answered, "The pain passes, but the pleasure, the creation of beauty, remains." One day when he was seventy-eight, finally quite famous and successful, he remarked, "I'm still making progress." The next day he died.

That's the mark of the creative person . . . still making progress, still learning, still producing, as long as he or she lives, despite pain or problems of all kinds. Creating because they *must*.

To a great extent, the challenges of our lives all involve similar obstacles. Goal achievement, wealth building, and public speaking are alike in many ways. All of them require effective decision making. The hard part is that we sometimes face what seems to be an endless list of possibilities. After all, the dictionary has lots of words from which you can construct your speech. The problem lies in choosing the right ones!

The first step in solving any problem is to define it, and this applies to the challenge of public speaking. You should always be sure you understand a problem before you go to work on its solution.

Next, you should write down everything you know about the problem. This information might come from your own experience, from books that contain background and statistical data, the Internet, or from friends and business associates who know something about the problem. It most definitely should come from this book!

Third, decide whom to see. List the names of people and organizations that are recognized authorities on the problem. This is your opportunity to go all out for the facts. After determining who can help you, contact them, talk with them, and pick their brains for all the information they possess.

Then be sure to make a note of each thing that's germane to the problem. Don't risk forgetting anything that could help you find the solution.

The fifth step in solving a problem creatively is called individual ideation. This is personal brainstorming, or thinking with the brakes of judgment off! Don't try to decide whether an idea is good or bad, just write it down the moment it comes to you. You can pick and choose later.

One idea often leads to another, better idea. Don't worry if some of your ideas seem far-fetched or impractical. You're looking for all the ideas you can possibly find. Don't reject any— write them all down!

When you have all your ideas written down, rate them for effectiveness and facility. The effectiveness scale ranges from "very effective" to "probably effective" to "doubtful." The facility scale ranges from "easy" to "not so easy" to "difficult." The rating of the ideas will clearly indicate the likely success of any possible solution. Consider first the idea or ideas that are rated both "very effective" and "easy."

Suppose you're a manufacturer. Suppose your sales and marketing teams' brainstorming comes up with some ideas to increase sales. Let's say one of the ideas is to revamp completely one of the products that your company is offering to the public. Let's rate this idea in terms of effectiveness. You know the present product meets a need and is acceptable to the buying public. What about an entirely changed product? Without a lot of marketing tests and then a period of actual manufacturing for sale, it would be hard to say just how effective this idea would be in increasing sales. Better rate it "doubtful."

How does this idea of completely revamping one of the products check out in the facility area—"easy," "not so easy," or "difficult"? It would be "difficult," wouldn't it? It would require new engineering, new tools, new manufacturing plans, new packaging, and new marketing methods.

Suppose, however, that one of the salesperson's ideas is to run TV advertisements for the company's product on one of the major television networks. This would be "probably effective" and would be "not so easy," but it could be done.

Let's say another idea is to set up a new sales-incentive program, directed to those who are at the front of the problem, the salespeople. A well-designed and well-implemented incentive program with predictable compensation for increased performance would stand a good chance of being "very effective." It would be relatively "easy" to do. It should increase the company's sales.

You might use many other evaluation yardsticks. Two more are time and money. Try rating your ideas against these measurements. For example, for the manufacturer who wants to increase sales, changing the product would take a great deal of time and money. To advertise it on a popular network television program would cost a great deal. On the other hand, introducing a new sales-incentive program might be neither too costly nor too time-consuming.

So remember, when you evaluate your ideas, measure them against these four yardsticks: effectiveness, facility, time, and cost. Not every idea you have will be worth creative action, and that's why you must skillfully evaluate each of them. But once you've carefully judged your ideas, take action.

Enter your ideas into an action plan: decide who should do it, when it should be done, when to start, and how to do it. These are all important considerations because the execution of the solution is just as important as the solution itself.

Give yourself a deadline for putting your plan into action. We work hardest and most efficiently when we have a definite time limit. So make a note of the date when you must put your solution to work. It's good to remember that timing is often critical when a new idea is introduced. Carefully calculate the deadline in the light of the general situation. You might write down a second date—the one by which you intend to have the action completed and the problem solved.

For any problem—no matter how big or complex—there is a solution. So go find it! History is filled with people who believed a problem did not have a solution and, as a consequence, *did not* find one. And people who believed there was a solution and *did* find it—same problem, different perspective, one successful and one not. Which type of person will you be with regard to your work in public speaking?

Developing yourself as a public speaker may be even more challenging than manufacturing or sales. The emotional side of being a successful speaker isn't so critical in other areas of business. Public speaking is extremely complex, and thousands of books have been written about it. But in addition to the fairly detailed techniques we've just discussed, an equally useful tool is surprisingly simple. In just the short time required to read this chapter, you can learn an absolutely surefire method for making your talk memorable for your audience and leading them to make immediate and positive changes based it. All this is made possible by the speaking technique that Dale Carnegie called the Magic Formula—and once you start using that technique, you'll see that it is exactly a magic formula.

The purpose of public speaking is to inspire action of some kind. A casual conversation in Starbucks may take place just to pass the time, but that's not our focus here. When you stand up in front of a group of people, you want them to do something. If they do it after hearing your talk, then the talk can be called a success. If you're making a business presentation, you may want an important new client to commit to a purchase. Or, if it's an internal presentation, you may be seeking authorization to form a project team or to develop a new product. These are common goals for formal talks and presentations, but even simple conferences or updates solicit someone to take action. So that solicitation has to be made effectively.

When public speaking is not effective, that's often because it hasn't been presented in the best possible format. We're going to address that issue in this chapter, first through the Magic Formula, then through three clear outlines that can be applied to virtually any public speaking situation. But one principle is fundamental to everything you're about to read. You need to begin your talks in a way that creates and holds the interest of the audience, and you need to end those talks in a way that is motivational and action-oriented.

So from the very beginning of a presentation, you should have the end in mind. In your own mind you should start with the action you want your listeners to take and work backward from there. Having done that, you're ready to connect with the Magic Formula, which will bring about the action you desire your listeners to take.

The Magic Formula first came into being when Dale Carnegie classes were just beginning to catch on across the country. Because of the size of classes, practice talks given by students were limited to two minutes. This did not affect the talk when the purpose of the speaker was merely to entertain or inform. But when the goal was to bring about action, two minutes just wasn't enough time, especially if a traditional format for the speech was put to use. A talk with an introduction, the body of the speech, and a conclusion couldn't get off the ground, yet this was the organizational pattern followed by speakers since ancient times. So something new and different was needed; it would have to be a surefire method for inspiring action with a two-minute speech.

To fill this need, Dale Carnegie instructors held meetings in Los Angeles, Chicago, and New York. Academic faculties and executives in major corporations were also consulted. From this diverse group, a new style of public speaking was about to emerge, a streamlined approach that would reflect our action-oriented age.

This was the Magic Formula. Like many potent ideas, it's deceptively simple and comprises just three clear steps.

First, you the speaker must share a vivid personal experience that's relevant to the action you ultimately want your listeners to take.

Second, call directly upon your audience to take that single, well-defined action.

Third, clearly and convincingly describe the benefit that listeners will gain by taking the action you desire.

In using the Magic Formula, you must make every word count. Used properly, this formula is suited to our contemporary way of life. It eliminates fluff and self-indulgence. The attention span of the modern audience is simply too short for those. People want action from you just as you want action from them, and with the Magic Formula, you give them action from the opening word.

Because it's based upon suspense, the formula is ideal for short talks. Listeners are caught up in your story, but they aren't aware of the point of your talk until the end of the two or three minutes. This is necessary for success in situations where you're making a significant demand of the audience. No speaker who wants people to dig deep in their pocketbooks will get far by starting, "Ladies and gentlemen, I'm here to collect five dollars from each of you." But if you dramatize the need you want to address with an incident from your own life, your chances of getting support hugely increase.

The first section of the Magic Formula—the incident from your own life—will take up the majority of your time. It should be a vivid description of an experience that taught you a lesson. As you prepare for telling this story, you should be aware that people learn lessons in two basic ways. The first is the so-called Law of Extension. This refers to a series of similar incidents leading to a change of our behavioral pattern. The alternative is the Law of Effect, in which a single event is so powerful as to cause a change in conduct.

In the example section of the formula, you must re-create a segment of your experience in such a way that it has the same effect upon your audience as it originally had upon you. You must clarify, intensify, and dramatize your experiences to make them compelling to your listeners.

Learning how to do this is not a matter of gaining new skills. What's needed is to remove blocks and impediments. As a professional speaker, your objective should be to talk with complete calm and naturalness, just as if you were with a close friend or relative.

Often in Dale Carnegie courses trainers will stop participants in the middle of a speech and remind them to talk like a regular human being—not as if a college professor or an international diplomat has somehow taken over their mind. Dale Carnegie himself put it, "So often I've come home tired out from trying to force my students to talk naturally. Believe me, it's not as easy as it sounds."

When you're telling a story from your life, especially a meaningful one, the only way to sound natural in front of an audience is through practice, both alone and in front of whatever audience you can pull together. As you practice, if you find yourself talking in a stilted manner, take a break and ask yourself what's wrong. Remind yourself of what's important in this kind of presentation. Use the technique of addressing yourself to another person, whether it's someone you envision or an actual member of the audience. Pick someone out—someone in the back, maybe the dullest-looking person you can find—and talk to that individual. Forget there's anyone else there at all.

Then just converse! Imagine you're answering a question from that person you've selected. If he or she were to stand up and talk to you, and you were to respond, you would immediately be more conversational, more natural, more direct. So imagine that's exactly what's taking place.

You may even want to externalize this by asking questions aloud during your speech. You can say something like "What did I think was going to happen next?" or "Why had I done something like that?" Then go ahead and answer the question. Although it may seem artificial, that sort of thing can be done naturally. It will break up any monotony in your delivery. It will make you sound direct and pleasant and conversational.

The goal in the first part of the Magic Formula is to put yourself totally under the influence of your feelings. When that happens, your real self comes to the surface. The barriers are down. The force of your emotion has broken through all of them. This comes back to something we've emphasized again and again in these chapters: put your heart in your talks.

Think of Christopher Reeve. When he became paralyzed from a riding accident, he became a spokesperson for people who were similarly challenged. When Congress was considering an appropriation to finance research for dealing with such ailments, Reeve appeared before the Senate Finance Committee and spoke about his accident. From his wheelchair, even though his paralysis had made him weak and sometimes difficult to understand, his message was powerfully clear. It came from deep within him. His heart was in his words.

His heart was in his words. That's the secret. Put your heart in your words when you tell your story. You can bore people if you talk about things or ideas, but you can hardly fail to hold their attention when you talk about something that's close to your heart. Every day, millions of conversations float over fences in backyards and over coffee tables and dinner tables—and what will be the predominant note in most of them? Human personalities. Stories about real human beings.

One Dale Carnegie student made this point clearly. She was a school administrator who had spoken with many groups of schoolchildren in the United States and Canada. As she described it, "I quickly learned that in order to keep them interested, I had to tell them stories about people. As soon as I began to generalize and deal with abstract ideas, some little girl would become restless and wiggly in her seat. Then a boy would make a face at somebody. And pretty soon another boy might even throw something across the room."

When a group of American business executives in Paris signed up for the Dale Carnegie effective-speaking course, their first exercise was a two-minute talk titled "How to Succeed." Most of them began by praising various homespun virtues. They preached at, lectured to, and bored their listeners. So the instructor halted the class and said, "We don't want to be lectured to. No one enjoys that. Remember, you have to be passionate and concise. Otherwise nobody's going to care what you're saying. It's that simple. Remember also that one of the most interesting things in the world is honest self-revelation. So tell us where you've been and who you are. Tell us about your successes and your failures. People will gladly hear that, remember it, and act on it. And by the way, it will actually be much easier for you to deliver than wordy preachments."

At one time public speaking was supposed to deal with generalities and so-called universal truths. That time is gone. The new rule is to deal with concrete facts that speak for themselves. An old-fashioned speaker might say that he was born of "poor but honest parents." A contemporary speaker might still speak of being poor, but if dishonesty also was part of his early life—well, he will need to be ruthlessly honest about that now.

Once you get in touch with the first part of the Magic Formula, you'll do more than just tell a story. You'll relive it, and the audience will live it with you. Your talk will actively engage your listeners rather than be just passively accepted. In this way you'll prepare them for the next step in the formula.

We've seen that a hard-hitting story of personal learning or transformation is the first stage of the Magic Formula. Having heard this, your listeners will be eager for you to tell what comes next, and they'll be disappointed if you don't. So now, in stage two, you're going to inform your audience exactly what action you want them to take. When I say *action*, that word is carefully chosen. The requested action needs to be specific and focused. It needs to be brief. When Christopher Reeve spoke to Congress, he didn't ask those elected officials to go out and change their lives. He didn't implore them to change the overall health care system. He didn't even ask for a general overhaul of the treatment of spinal-cord injuries. Instead, he just spoke about a single bill that would increase funding for research.

This is the key to stage two of the formula. Make your appeal as brief and as tangible as you possibly can. Put yourself in the place of someone appearing before a committee as Christopher Reeve did. For maximum effect, you shouldn't even speak of passing the bill. Your emphasis should be much more short-sighted, or even microscopic. Talk about "picking up the pen and putting the ink on the paper." Nothing abstract. Nothing preachy. Nothing that a child could not fully understand. Above all, this should seem like something that's *easy to do*. Take the thoughts of your listeners off the implications of what you're asking. Put their thoughts on the simple physical action. And do it with force and conviction.

For a good example of this, think of astronaut Neil Armstrong's famous statement when he first walked on the moon: "That's one small step for [a] man . . ." His emphasis was on the everyday physical action. He grounded the moment in something that everyone could relate to. Once he'd done that, the rest of the statement flowed naturally. "One giant leap for mankind" would have seemed preachy and pretentious if he had not first laid the everyday foundation.

This part of the formula should not take much time at all. Remember, the original need was for a format that could be executed within two minutes. You're trying to minimize what's being asked in stage two. That should be expressed by both the time it takes and the number of words you say. Less is more in stage two of the Magic Formula.

Now it's time for the third and final stage. It may be helpful to think of this as the mirror image of stage two, because now, instead of telling listeners what you want them to do, you tell them what they're going to get. You show them the huge benefit that they'll reap based on the simple action you've asked of them. Now, please notice that I said *benefit*—singular rather than plural. This is not a game show where you're promised a new car *plus* a washing machine *and* a Hawaiian vacation for two. People can't relate to that in a business or professional setting. Just make it clear that when the action you solicited is performed, a single major benefit will accrue to the audience. If the bill Christopher Reeves supported was passed, the legislators would be recognized for having done something extremely positive. That's all they had to be told. They were smart enough to understand how that recognition could translate into votes in the next election.

So let's summarize the correct use of the Magic Formula. This is a technique for creating connection, motivation, inspiration, and action in your audience in the shortest possible time. Have the three parts of the formula clearly in mind: first, the personal story that describes a positive change in your life. It can be a change that took place over time, or it may have happened quite suddenly, as a result of some turning-point event. You should relate this event with passion and energy. Ideally, you should almost relive it, so that your audience will live it with you. Of the three components of the formula, your personal story should definitely require the largest amount of time. At the end of it, listeners should be energized, engaged, and eager to learn where you are now going to take them.

Part two of the formula should take much less time than your personal story, but almost because it's so short, it should be equally hard-hitting. This is when you ask the audience to take a single, tangible, positive action, and it should flow naturally from the personal story they've just heard. If you need funds for a philanthropic endeavor, for instance, ask them to write a check, but ask them to do it right then and there, and keep the focus on the physical action. In their own minds, let *them* make the connection between this action and your story. If you've told the story effectively, that's exactly what they'll do. And if you haven't told it effectively, trying to salvage it now won't work. Just keep it simple and clear. In the fewest possible words, ask for the positive action you want them to take.

The third part of the formula may not take much longer than the second, but now you're helping the audience to look through the other end of the telescope. The time for the third stage is short, but the focus is much broader. Now you're going to tell listeners about the benefit they'll gain by taking the action you've asked for. Ideally, you refer specifically to only one benefit, but it should be broad enough so that people see why it's important and worthwhile. For example, if in stage two you asked a group of students to sign up for a summer school course, in stage three you tell them that this will assure them of college admission. You don't need to say anything more. In just a few words you paint the picture of a single major benefit that has broad implications.

Use this technique, practice it, and you'll see that it's called the Magic Formula for good reason.

The Magic Formula you've just learned is a framework for public speaking that has served thousands of participants in the Dale Carnegie organization. With a little practice, it will make you into a polished speaker in the shortest possible time. But to optimize the formula and the other tools we've introduced, you can't ignore the practical, physical setting in which your talk will take place, or the things you need in that setting for the talk to succeed. We'll conclude this chapter with a quick look at exactly what this involves.

Early on the morning of your talk, or last thing the night before, run through the presentation once more. Use a mirror or visualize standing in front of an audience as you practice.

If possible, early in the day take a tour of the room you'll use for the presentation. Look for potential problems with lines of sight or intrusive sounds. These all can be fixed with a bit of prior warning and a polite request to the organizers. If you're using audiovisual aids, such as a slide carousel, make sure they're properly set up. If you need any additional equipment, ask for it now. If you're not the one who will be controlling it during the speech, determine who will be performing that task for you.

Many if not most of today's presentations include computer use, and many if not most suffer some sort of breakdown along the way, often at the most inopportune moments. Here are a few potential issues to consider sooner rather than later.

Is the host software compatible with your presentation? Are the fonts, bullets, and colors all the same?

Is there a sound card in the host computer? Is the sound system operational, but not too loud?

Back up your presentation in an alternative laptop, then bring it with you separately from the one you plan to use. Or e-mail it to yourself as an attachment—you should be able to access it from the site of your talk.

If the room is large, be prepared to use a microphone. Try it out before the audience arrives. Check to see that any other needed accessories are ready, for example, a dry board, markers, eraser, and pointer. If it's a laser pointer, does it have fresh batteries loaded? Keep in mind that lasers quickly use up battery power. When writing on flip charts, use no more than seven lines of text per page, and no more than seven words per line. Also, use bright and bold colors. Create diagrams and pictures as well as text.

Don't be afraid to insist on a few minutes to yourself prior to the talk—fifteen to thirty minutes is standard. Use this time to double-check your materials, and your introductory and summary statements. Don't allow yourself to be distracted by audience members coming up to chat.

If possible, avoid standing behind a lectern or desk during the presentation. Stand to one side of the projection screen or blackboard, and closer to the audience if possible. If you have handouts, don't read from them during the talk. The audience won't know whether to read along with you or listen to you read.

Speak to the audience. Don't appear to be speaking to the visual aids such as flip charts or overheads. Also, do not stand between the visual aid and the audience. Speak clearly and loudly enough for all to hear. If possible, consider circulating around the room as you speak. This movement creates a physical closeness to the audience. Ideally, you should be prepared to use an alternative speaking approach if the one you've chosen seems to bog down. You should be confident enough with your material so that the audience's interests and concerns—not the presentation outline—determine the format you use.

Be aware of the time of day and how long you have for your talk. Time of day can affect the audience. Most speakers find that if they practice in their head, the actual talk will take about 25 percent longer. Using a flip chart or other visual aids also adds to the time. Remember that it's better to finish slightly early than to overrun.

In the next chapter we'll discuss how to handle questions and answers, but you should always listen closely to any audience comments. Even if you disagree, try building on ideas rather than contradicting them. Finally, just as you should get to the presentation site before the audience arrives, you should also be the last one to leave.

A successful talk depends on good logistical planning and execution. In our next chapter we'll see how, even if everything goes smoothly, public speaking can still involve pressure, and sometimes even outright disagreement or conflict with listeners. A key test of a speaker is his or her ability to handle those moments with poise and patience.

Franklin Delano Roosevelt

Excerpt from Franklin D. Roosevelt's first fireside chat:

I want to talk for a few minutes with the people of the United States about banking—with the comparatively few who understand the mechanics of banking but more particularly with the overwhelming majority who use banks for the making of deposits and the drawing of checks. I want to tell you what has been done in the last few days, why it was done, and what the next steps are going to be. I recognize that the many proclamations from State Capitols and from Washington, the legislation, the Treasury regulations, etc., couched for the most part in banking and legal terms, should be explained for the benefit of the average citizen. I owe this in particular because of the fortitude and good temper with which everybody has accepted the inconvenience and hardships of the banking holiday. I know that when you understand what we in Washington have been about I shall continue to have your cooperation as fully as I have had your sympathy and help during the past week.

First of all let me state the simple fact that when you deposit money in a bank the bank does not put the money into a safe deposit vault. It invests your money in many different forms of credit-bonds, commercial paper, mortgages and many other kinds of loans. In other words, the bank puts your money to work to keep the wheels of industry and of agriculture turning around. A comparatively small part of the money you put into the bank is kept in currency—an amount which in normal times is wholly sufficient to cover the cash needs of the average citizen. In other words the total amount of all the currency in the country is only a small fraction of the total deposits in all of the banks.

What, then, happened during the last few days of February and the first few days of March? Because of undermined confidence on the part of the public, there was a general rush by a large portion of our population to turn bank deposits into currency or gold—a rush so great that the soundest banks could not get enough currency to meet the demand. The reason for this was that on the spur of the moment it was, of course, impossible to sell perfectly sound assets of a bank and convert them into cash except at panic prices far below their real value.

By the afternoon of March 3 scarcely a bank in the country was open to do business. Proclamations temporarily closing them in whole or in part had been issued by the Governors in almost all the states.

It was then that I issued the proclamation providing for the nationwide bank holiday, and this was the first step in the Government's reconstruction of our financial and economic fabric.

Roosevelt was elected for his first term at a time when the country was in the depths of a horrendous depression. Thirteen million people were unemployed, and the vast majority of banks were closed. Roosevelt needed to find an effective way to communicate with the country, to encourage and uplift his people.

On March 12, 1933, President Roosevelt gave his first fireside chat, a radio address in which he explained to the nation how we were going to recover from the current banking crisis.

It was the first of thirty-one historic fireside chats that Roosevelt would give. His voice was always calm and reassuring as he discussed a wide variety of issues and encouraged the American people to tell him their troubles.

Roosevelt was keenly aware of who his audience was, and he took great care to make his chats understandable to everyday Americans. He used basic language, going so far as to make sure that the vast majority of the words he used were among the thousand most commonly used words in the English vocabulary.

Roosevelt's speaking style was conversational, relying on stories and anecdotes to clarify the complicated issues facing the country. He often referred to his listeners as "you" and "we," thereby encouraging a sense of intimacy between the public and the president.

The White House was deluged with letters from all types of Americans who responded positively to Roosevelt's fireside chats. Many of them felt that when they heard their president on the radio, it was as if he were talking to them personally in their homes.

Through the radio, and with his carefully prepared and delivered chats, Roosevelt connected with the public in a way no other president ever has before or since.

Excerpt from Franklin D. Roosevelt's first fireside chat:

We had a bad banking situation. Some of our bankers had shown themselves either incompetent or dishonest in their handling of the people's funds. They had used the money entrusted to them in speculations and unwise loans. This was of course not true in the vast

*majority of our banks but it was true in enough of them to shock the
people for a time into a sense of insecurity and to put them into a
frame of mind where they did not differentiate, but seemed to assume
that the acts of a comparative few had tainted them all. It was the
Government's job to straighten out this situation and do it as quickly
as possible—and the job is being performed.*

*I do not promise you that every bank will be reopened or that indi-
vidual losses will not be suffered, but there will be no losses that possibly could be avoided; and there would have been more and greater
losses had we continued to drift. I can even promise you salvation
for some at least of the sorely pressed banks. We shall be engaged not
merely in reopening sound banks but in the creation of sound banks
through reorganization. It has been wonderful to me to catch the
note of confidence from all over the country. I can never be sufficiently
grateful to the people for the loyal support they have given me in their
acceptance of the judgment that has dictated our course, even though
all of our processes may not have seemed clear to them.*

*After all there is an element in the readjustment of our financial
system more important than currency, more important than gold, and
that is the confidence of the people. Confidence and courage are the
essentials of success in carrying out our plan. You people must have
faith; you must not be stampeded by rumors or guesses. Let us unite in
banishing fear. We have provided the machinery to restore our financial system; it is up to you to support and make it work.*

It is your problem no less than it is mine. Together we cannot fail.

He who wants to persuade should put his trust not in the right argument, but in the right word. The power of sound has always been greater than the power of sense.

—Joseph Conrad

It's not how strongly you feel about your topic, it's how strongly they feel about your topic after you speak.

—Tim Salladay

If you can't write your message in a sentence, you can't say it in an hour.

—Dianna Booher

CHAPTER 11

Dealing with Questions and Answers

Regardless of how long or short your presentation might be, the most important parts are the beginning and the end, but what exactly defines the end of a talk? Simply put, your speech isn't over when you've finished what you have to say. Once you've reached that point, most speakers then invite questions from listeners, and often this is the most influential and memorable part of the talk.

A question-and-answer period is both a challenge and an opportunity. You now have a chance to clarify your message, to reinforce key points, and to bring any resistance out into the open. The downside is that some questions can be difficult to answer, especially if you're not well prepared. It's also not unusual for a single questioner to dominate the discussion, or at least to try to dominate it. Some audiences are shy or nonresponsive. And occasionally an audience can be outright hostile.

Most question-and-answer periods follow a clear pattern. Applause will generally follow your presentation. Then you can say, "I have x amount of time for questions and answers. Who has the first question?" An expectant look on your face will cue the audience as to what comes next. Every question-and-answer period should begin with your setting a time limit. Sometimes you may want to make this specific, especially if your talk has run a bit long. You can say "five minutes" or "ten minutes." But most often it's best to leave it a bit vague. Just say, "We have a few minutes for Q and A." Even if plenty of time is available, you certainly don't want to say, "I have two hours to take your questions." You and everybody else would be sorry!

Clearly communicating how much time will be allowed for the Q & A helps to keep the questions short and to the point, and your answers should also be concise. You may occasionally want to spend more time on an individual answer, especially if it's a point you weren't able to develop in the talk itself.

During the Q & A, your ability to interact one-on-one with the audience is going to be evaluated. Since you can't always predict what you'll be asked, how can you be prepared for this?

A good place to start is by getting your listening skill into shape. Whether you know it or not, listening is a skill just as much as speaking is. Because many presenters don't realize that, they're much less adept at hearing others than they are at speaking themselves. But you can't answer a question well if you haven't heard it correctly. So please study the following listening problems carefully. These are just a few of the issues that often come up, but they'll give you an idea of things you need to watch out for.

Number one—interrupting the questioner. Sometimes presenters are very convinced of their own wisdom. As a result, they're not able to meet audience members where they are in their understanding. Speakers lose patience and interrupt. This can seriously damage your cause, much more so than if you'd at least listened to the whole question and then given a weak answer.

There is only one exception to this. Sometimes it may be

necessary to break in on a vague, rambling question. This is your presentation and you have only a limited time for it. But it's essential that you break in tactfully. Say something like "So, are you asking . . . ?" This will focus the question and give you a place to begin an answer. Remember that your ability to interact with an audience is also being evaluated. It's not just what you say, but how you handle the side issues as well.

Number two—not looking at the speaker. Eye contact is just as important during the Q & A as it was during the talk. When someone speaks up, give your full attention to the question. Show respect for the questioner by looking as well as listening. One without the other just doesn't work. When you're certain that the questioner is finished, pause for thought. Don't be in a hurry to start talking. You may be tempted to do this, especially if the question was hostile. But take your time. In addition to being polite, pausing for thought can help your credibility too. The message will be that you are taking the person seriously as you carefully consider his or her question.

Now look at the person asking the question and repeat it—not word for word, but in paraphrase. This is especially important if there is a large audience that might not have heard everything clearly. By repeating the question you also insure you understood what the person asked.

When you actually start to respond to the question, break eye contact with the questioner and address the audience as a whole. Remember that you are still in a public speaking situation and all the listeners should hear your answer—not just the one who asked the question. Remain in a neutral position where you are equally distant from all members of your audience. Avoid the temptation to move or speak directly to the person who asked the question. Visually this will make the rest of the audience feel left out.

Listening problem number three—rushing questioners and making them feel that they're wasting your time. What's the hurry? They've listened to you for an extended period. Now it's your turn to listen for a moment. Don't get so used to talking that you can't do anything else. And as you begin to make your response, try to keep your answer concise and to the point. Don't give another presentation. The audience will be bored or even resentful if you take too long to answer a particular question. In addition, it's possible that the only person interested in the answer is the one who asked it in the first place!

Number four—blatantly not answering the question. As we'll see later in this chapter, you have ways to get your core message across in a Q & A regardless of what you're asked. But this needs to be done with finesse. You can't just ignore a question and reprise your speech.

Number five is especially common and unfortunate. The questioner has related an incident or anecdote, and you ignore that material and try to top it with a story of your own. Usually this begins with a phrase like "That reminds me . . ." or "Let me tell you about . . ." If you hear those words coming out of your mouth during a Q & A, check yourself immediately. You're headed in the wrong direction.

Number six—leading, loaded, and digressive questions. Whether they intend to or not, listeners can lay traps with questions that will get you into deep water if you don't correctly respond. For example, you may be presented with what's known as a leading question. Leading questions are those that tempt, urge, or even shove you toward a certain answer while ignoring other possibilities. So-called closed questions are especially loaded in this way. An example might be "Do you think the CEO is having problems?" Note how an affirmative answer is implied in the question itself. A more extreme example might be "Do you think the CEO's problems are worse than ever before?" With leading questions of this kind, the best choice is always to disagree and then follow with an explanation. Saying yes commits you to an extreme position, so that anything further you might say can seem irrelevant.

Don't answer a leading question directly. Think about it and defuse it before you respond. Suppose someone asks, "What are you doing with all the money you are making from increased prices?" Defuse the hostility by saying, "I understand your frustration with the recent rate increase. I think what you're really asking is, 'Why such a sudden increase in rates?'" Then answer that question instead of the leading and loaded one.

Conflict happens only when you allow yourself to answer a loaded question. If the questioner isn't satisfied with your response, suggest that you'll be glad to talk about it following the Q & A. Then move quickly to the next question.

Once the questions really start coming, you face a lot of possibilities. Sometimes, under the guise of asking a question, a listener will try to make an extended comment or even a whole speech. The question turns into an interrogation. The questioner just goes on and on, to the point that you feel like leaving, at least psychologically. Then, when you finally get a chance to answer, the person instantly fires back with another question. You've got to be prepared for this and know how to handle it.

For your own sake and that of the other people in the

audience, you'll need to be firm. You may have to interrupt to say, "What is your question?" That will usually be enough to hurry things up. Then it's best to respond briefly, especially if the long-winded comment was delivered with hostility. By giving a brief answer, you can keep the total amount of time you've spent with this person in line with what you've given other audience members. Don't let yourself get drawn into a long response or rebuttal.

If you choose to respond to the follow-up question, that's usually okay, but then simply call on someone else. Don't explain and don't apologize. Just do it. The audience will understand and will probably be grateful as well.

Sometimes negativity in questions can trigger unintentional negativity in your answers. Take a typical question like "What problems have you had recently?" This contains the built-in notion that you've had problems all along, but now we're just going to talk about the ones that you've recently had. The word *problem* can tip you into thinking negatively.

The digressive question offers another kind of temptation. This is a question that can lead you away from your true area of interest. It can launch you into a reminiscence about something that may suddenly seem interesting to you, but is not really in line with what your audience wants to hear about. This can be costly in the time you have available and in the attention of your listeners.

I think you can see how leading questions can lead you into temptation. But nonleading questions can also be problematic. Instead of tempting you to say too much or to say something inappropriate, some questions are so bland that you don't know what to say at all. Often these questions come from listeners who are nervous about speaking up. The question they ask is meaningful to them, but what's really meaningful is the intensity of just asking it in public. The question itself is often simple or simplistic. When this happens, it's often a good idea to seek more detail. Ask something like "What exactly did you mean by such and such?" or "Could you tell me more about so-and-so?" One of the most effective ways of getting more detail is simply by asking the same question again. You can use the same words or you can rephrase it, perhaps with emphasis on the area where you want more information.

It sometimes happens that no one asks a question at all. Most often this just means that listeners aren't sure how safe it is to speak up. Ironically, this is most likely to happen when your presentation was especially strong. Now your task is to prime the pump. You could say, for instance, "Something that's often asked is . . ." After you've responded to the hypothetical question, you then say, "Who has something else?" Don't panic if there are a few seconds of silence. Your listeners will want to fill that silence as much as you do. But if nothing is forthcoming, ask and answer another hypothetical question. Two is enough. If there's nothing further, thank the audience for their attention, repeat the closing point of your talk in one sentence, and simply shut off your microphone or step away from the podium. You're done. This will rarely be necessary, but it's always good to be prepared. Usually there are many more questions than there is time, especially after someone has gotten the ball rolling.

To deal with these common issues and other pitfalls that come up in Q & A sessions, you should practice listening just as you practice speaking. And as your skills improve, you'll learn to recognize certain patterns in people's questions that will make them easier to deal with.

Experienced speakers know how to stay on message no matter what the distraction. This is an important skill to learn. As part of your overall preparation for your talk, you should have a small number of key phrases and central ideas that you truly want to get across. These should be part of the speech itself, but the Q & A is an especially good place to hammer these sound bites home. With practice, you'll be able to do this gracefully regardless of what a given questioner actually asks. This is not being evasive but rather taking every opportunity to say what you want to say.

No matter what you may be thinking, don't evaluate questions. Avoid saying "Good question" or "That's a great question." If the next person doesn't get thrown a similar bone, it may seem that you somehow disapprove. This could stifle others from speaking up. If you want to affirm what people ask, just say, "Thanks for your question." Make everyone feel equally good about what he or she asks.

It's often a good idea to answer a question with some surprising new information, or in a way that alters the spin of your original talk. Rather than give the answer that people expect, change tack with something outside your normal range. Be candid. Be frank. Break with custom. Tell the truth as you see it even when it might not be expected. Even if your answer might provoke disagreement, be disarmingly honest. You won't damage your credibility as long as your response seems to have some thought behind it.

Showering questioners with details can sometimes be a good tactic. Probably the best at this is former president Bill Clinton.

He was always at his best in Q & A sessions, and a number of them were televised during his administration. His mastery of detailed information was always impressive, regardless of whether you agreed with what he said.

If you're uncomfortable with answering a certain question, you can always respond with a question of your own. This can be an honest attempt to gain more information, or it can be a delaying tactic to gain more time. If the exchange becomes more confrontational, you can become more aggressive while still remaining under control. Challenge the question that's been asked. Suggest that other questions are more important or should be asked first. If you feel it's justified and necessary, you can even challenge the legitimacy of the questioner. You can say, "How are you even authorized to ask that?" Then follow up by asking a completely different question of your own—and answering it. These are extreme measures, but as a high impact speaker you must be prepared for a variety of responses to your ideas. Handling conflict correctly displays your knowledge and professionalism. But always retain your poise, and never let your anger show. Even if what you say would sound angry if you read it on a printed page, keep your voice even and your temper under control. Be up-front with a questioner if you think the inquiry is not relevant. Your response might be "Actually, that question doesn't the fit the context of our discussion." Work hard not to lose your temper with a person who is trying to make you look bad. As someone once said, "He who grins wins." This is absolutely true of Q & A sessions.

Whenever you open your presentation for audience participation, you always risk unexpected responses. So anticipate the unexpected. Plan ahead as much as possible. Look at your content and think about likely questions the audience will ask. Prepare your own questions to ask. Don't be afraid to say, "I don't know," and move on to the next question. You can add that you will be glad to get back to the person with an answer later.

The Dale Carnegie organization has always been honest about facing certain key facts about human nature. We are continually trying to win other people over to our way of thinking. This is especially true during oral presentations, and even more so when taking questions. The first step in a Q & A should be understanding what's on other people's minds and looking for a common ground of agreement. Answers flow easily when you and the questioner are in sync in some way and when you display a sincere interest in what that person is trying to express. This sincere interest will have a far more lasting impression than any verbal blunder you might make. Yet most of us are more interested in unloading our own opinions before we do anything else. You've got to get beyond that point if you aspire to be a high impact speaker.

Flat-out defiance of a hostile questioner is always a difficult handicap for a speaker to overcome. Once you've entered that mode, all your pride of personality demands that you remain consistent with yourself. Later you may feel that the stance you adopted was ill-advised, but for the moment you'll be stuck with it. So don't go there in the first place. Think about what you're doing and saying rather than just reacting to what's being said to you.

One of the greatest mistakes you can make as a professional is to lose your composure in a pressure situation, especially when your talk involves important issues. Even if your outward composure doesn't obviously falter, you never want it to appear that you have anything but the highest confidence in your ideas, in your ability to present them, and in yourself as well. With practice and experience, you can handle situations in which difficult or even potentially embarrassing questions arise.

Interestingly, a positive, confident speaker creates confidence in the questioner as well. Emotions and attitudes are catching. If you are uncertain in your arguments and appear to lack belief in yourself, how can the questioner be persuaded? We all have a need for certainty, and confidence is the outward sign of this quality in yourself. Confidence, therefore, is a message in itself. A nonconfident person who is trying to convince others is sending a mixed signal. For listeners to be confident in their decision to agree with you, all of your messages—verbal and nonverbal—must be in alignment.

So confidence starts with yourself. How is that displayed? Being brash and combative is often a sign of someone who lacks confidence and is trying to compensate for this. A much more powerful approach is to be firm and forceful, but also to embrace the challenge of being open when you are uncertain about a specific point. At times, "I just don't know" is the best answer, especially when it's obvious that you really don't.

Each time you answer a question, whether it's a good one or a bad one, always finish your answer by asking if your response was sufficient. This acknowledges and thanks the questioner, it lets the rest of the audience feel comfortable asking questions, and it gives you a chance to more fully answer the question if your first effort was not quite on target. If the questioner says you didn't answer the question and you believe you did, either ask the person to clarify the question or suggest that the two of you can go into more detail later. Remember that many speaking situations involve two presentations: the formal presentation and the Q & A. You can insure success for *both* presentations by using the techniques we've discussed.

In the previous chapter we discussed some concerns raised by incorporating high technology in your presentation. A few such issues are related to the question-and-answer period. For example, if you've been projecting slides or images from a computer, select the one that you feel is most striking or informative and leave it on the screen while you take questions. This will keep your key information in the forefront of your listeners' minds. It can also help guide the flow of the Q & A portion of your speech.

You should project this image as soon as the body of your speech ends. Avoid turning off the projector or the computer because you'll just have to turn it on again and wait while it boots up. Leaving a dazzling white screen or blank black slide is definitely not a good idea. At best it's uninteresting, and at worst it's a distraction.

One final thought. Some experienced speakers save the conclusion of their talk until after the Q & A. This allows you to control exactly when your time in front of the audience will end. Instead of everyone, including you, wondering when the last question will come, the audience receives your prepared conclusion when you choose. To make this happen, you might say, "Before I make some concluding remarks, who has a question to ask?" Then after you take the amount of time you want for the Q & A, go to the podium for your conclusion. In this way, you can end on a positive, proactive note instead of trailing off with "So if there are no further questions, I guess that's it."

But that isn't it. We have one more chapter to go!

The most precious things in speech are the pauses.

—Sir Ralph Richardson

To be a person is to have a story to tell.

—Isak Dinesen

Speak clearly, if you speak at all; carve every word before you let it fall.

—Oliver Wendell Holmes

CHAPTER 12

How to Conclude a Presentation

As a highly effective public speaker, you need to close your presentations by leaving your audience something of special value. The impact of your speech as a whole depends on your ability to end it with meaning and with passion. To do this, you'll need to provide information that your listeners can use to improve their lives. How can you be certain to do that? The answers are here in chapter 12.

The beginning and the ending of a speech are the hardest elements to manage gracefully. While the opening of a presentation should add up to a positive first impression, the conclusion should add up to a positive lasting impression. The beginning is most important in establishing a connection with the audience for the time they will be listening, but the end, hopefully, is something they will remember forever. So why is it that so many speakers come to such an unsatisfying close? "Well, that's about all I have to say, so I guess I'll wind it up." That's not an ending in any meaningful sense. It would be better to just stop talking and take a seat.

A good ending to a presentation doesn't happen by itself. It has to be carefully planned. Even the most accomplished speakers—men and women whose command of the language is impeccable—have all felt it necessary to write down the exact words of their closings. They did not memorize these words, but they read them and studied them to such a degree that, when the time came, they spoke naturally and with absolute conviction.

If you're just starting out, you should absolutely follow this model. You should know what words to use in your conclusion, and what the effect of those words will be. Then rehearse again and again from memory, not focusing on using the same exact words during each repetition, but on putting the same thoughts into whatever words you use. It's usually better to speak your conclusion without reading it. If you're more comfortable using notes, put them in bullet form, listing the main ideas you want to reiterate and reinforce from your presentation. Keeping your eyes on your audience instead of your notes is always helpful, the more so when your conclusion is a call to action.

Some speakers never get to the end of their talk at all. Somewhere in the middle they just begin circling around. Then they either stop too abruptly or go on too long. Even in a short talk of three to five minutes a speaker is apt to cover so much ground that at the close the listeners are hazy about all the main points. Inexperienced presenters may assume that their points are crystal clear in the minds of the listeners because they're crystal clear to the speaker. The speaker, however, has been working on these ideas for weeks, or even months. But they're new to the audience. Hearing them for the first time, listeners are likely to remember a lot of things vaguely, but little distinctly.

For this reason, one of the worst mistakes you can make as a public speaker is talking too long. It doesn't matter if your talk was brilliant and the audience received information that could change their lives. If your talk is too long, their comment will be "That speaker just wouldn't quit." Don't let this happen to you! Say what you have to say and sit down. But just before you do, give the audience a well-thought-out closing.

Since the last thing you say will be the best remembered, you must put serious effort into selecting and practicing your closing. Make your final impression a lasting one. Think about how you can make your conclusion memorable both in substance and delivery. You can use a variety of the techniques from your successful speaker's toolbox. Consider, for example, combining intonation, pauses, and especially to-the-point phrases that are likely to stay with your audience. Jack Welch, in his early days as CEO of General Electric, faced the need for radical changes in the company's business direction. He would often end meetings with a simple call to the company's employees: "Change before you have to." The message behind that sound bite was unmistakable and eventually resonated throughout the company. It was the best and most successful summation of Welch's business philosophy.

Your ending can be motivational, challenging, thoughtful, respectful, or humorous—but it had better be good, because it *will* be memorable. A humorous close has several advantages. If you leave the audience laughing and applauding, an extremely positive impression of you will remain. Anything else risks polite applause or even silence as you move away from the podium.

Nobody wants that. So let's see how you can optimize the conclusion of your talk. Start by asking some questions about your presentation. For example, was the speech developed in a simple or a complex fashion? If it was short and sweet, there may not be a need to sum things up. But if the ideas were more complicated, offer a summary in the conclusion just as you gave a road map at the beginning. Remind the audience of your major themes. For example, here's a summary from a talk about advanced-placement classes in high schools:

"Today I have tried to show you that AP classes should be expanded and encouraged as much as possible. I first explained that such classes are a distinguishing feature of virtually all high-performing schools. Second, I made the point that advance-placement classes contribute directly to success in college admissions. Finally, I documented that AP classes are linked to better scores on standardized tests, and thus to a higher standard of education throughout the country."

In some speeches you may think this is too mechanical. You may choose to paraphrase rather than restate exactly, summing up the content in the fewest possible words. But always keep in mind that for a summary to be effective, there must already be information in the minds of the listeners. You can't rebuild what has not been built in the first place. The effectiveness of your close is a function of your speech as a whole. The foundation has to be in place before the flag can be raised on top of the building.

Sometimes a talk may have advanced only one major idea, an idea that is inspirational rather than informational. Then you need only a simple, powerful restatement of the central point to ensure audience understanding. But you need to make it really memorable.

Whether it's designed to inspire or to inform, a successful ending always conveys a sense of completeness, finality, and control. You can assert this sense of control by using transition phrases to foreshadow the end of your talk. You might say "In summary . . ." or "As I conclude this address . . ." or "Let me re-iterate . . ." The degree you should do this will depend on your experience and confidence as a speaker. Early on, the best thing is to stick to the tried-and-true rules of presentation. Later you can bend the rules. Ultimately, you can become one of the master speakers who are able to make their own rules.

In our discussion of Dale Carnegie's Magic Formula in chapter 10, we saw the importance of asking for a distinct, clearly defined action from your audience. Although the Magic Formula is most appropriate for short presentations, it's always good to openly appeal for support, or to remind listeners of their responsibilities in furthering a desirable end. Be vivid and compelling—and include a suggestion of the principle ideas or arguments presented in your speech.

Read this conclusion from a speech by President Harry Truman urging Congress to authorize funds for aid to other countries.

"This is a serious course upon which we embark. I would not recommend it except that the alternative is even more serious. We must invest in world freedom and world peace. The seeds of totalitarian regimes are nurtured by misery and want. They spread and grow in the evil soil of poverty and strife. They reach their full growth when the hope of a people for a better life has died. We must keep that hope alive. If we falter in our leadership, we may endanger the peace of the world. And we shall surely endanger the welfare of this nation. I am confident that the Congress will face these responsibilities squarely."

Along similar, action-oriented lines, Robert Kennedy spoke these words during his senatorial campaign in New York State:

"For us, the responsibility is clear. We must reject the counsel of those willing to pass laws against violence while refusing to help eliminate rats in people's homes. We must offer leadership that dares to speak out before it tests the shifting wind of popular anger and confusion. Leadership that prefers facts to illusions, actions to sullen withdrawal, sacrifice and effort to indulgence and ease."

If you used a quotation at the beginning of your presentation, you can tie the speech together by a reference back to the earlier quote. Suppose you began with the quote "Most ignorance is chosen ignorance. We don't know because we don't want to know." In your conclusion you can spin the same idea in an opposite direction: "The cure of our not knowing is our wanting to know."

Any speech-ending illustration should be both inclusive and conclusive. It should be inclusive of the main focus of your speech and conclusive in tone and impact. One speaker used the same image in both the opening and the closing of his speech on the causes and effects of poverty.

Here's the opening:

"Have you ever felt like you were that little Dutch boy who stuck his finger in the leaking dike? You waited and waited but the help never came. The leak became worse and the water rushed around you and swept you away. As you fought the flood, you realized that the flood was inside yourself. You were drowning and dying in your own life. The fact is, as many as three-quarters of the people in the world will be carried away by this devastating flood. What is this disaster? World poverty."

And here's the conclusion:

"Let's go back to my illustration of the little Dutch boy. He was wise to take action and put his finger in the dike, preventing the flood. In the case of poverty, each one of us must be like that boy—willing to get involved to control the catastrophic effects of poverty."

Throughout this presentation, the speaker had discussed at length the effects of poverty in his own family. Besides tying the introduction and conclusion together, this speaker also added an inducement:

"Why should you really care? Why is it important? The people who will be helped could be someone you know. It could even be you. My family wasn't saved. I hope it's never necessary, but perhaps someday yours will be."

When you use your conclusion to ask listeners for action, it's a good idea to state your own intent. A college student ended her speech on fear of flying with her solution:

"Although it is still difficult for me to get on an airplane, I am convinced it is worth my while. I believe all of us should take the risk required to overcome irrational fears. Only in that way will we be able to fully take part in the contemporary world. I've got a ticket to Miami for tomorrow morning. I hope to see you down there."

All these strategies can be effective provided they're used in a controlled and organized manner. Be sure, for instance, to leave enough time in your speech for a solid conclusion. If you are running short on time, don't cut from the end, since psychologically this is the strongest part of your talk. Just as you did in your introduction, build your presence in the conclusion with solid, confident nonverbal cues. Look at the audience. Be personal. Be energetic. Take the time to plan a solid conclusion, and make sure you don't give your listeners a false sense of when you will finish. Few things annoy an audience as much as thinking a speech is over, only to have the speaker go on and on. So don't use the phrases *in conclusion* or *in summary* in any part of the speech other than the actual conclusion. You will lose part of your audience as they realize that the speech is continuing even though they thought it was winding down.

Here are some other conclusion pitfalls to avoid:

Do not use *thank you* as a substitute for a powerful closing phrase. It's impossible to imagine Dr. King or President Kennedy or even Bill Gates ending a speech with *thank you*. The idea of Lincoln or Theodore Roosevelt doing so is positively laughable. Think of a phrase that summarizes your thesis in the fewest possible words, something that will stay in the heads of your audience not only for the time it takes to reach the parking lot, but for a long time to come. Close with that phrase. Your listeners will be thankful that you did so, don't worry about thanking them.

You shouldn't start a speech with an apology, so don't end with one either. "I guess I've rambled on long enough." "I don't know if I've made this clear, but I'm stopping here." "I hope I haven't bored you too much." Hundreds of these apologetic phrases are floating around that people use to finish their speeches. While they seem to be self-depreciating, they're really a way speakers can congratulate themselves for their humility. They're also an attempt to disarm any criticism from listeners by beating them to the punch. A good speaker has more class than that, and if you've gotten this far in the book, you're well on your way to being a good speaker.

Don't make the conclusion disproportionately long. Don't introduce a whole new idea in your conclusion. That runs the risk of confusing your audience and obscuring your original message. In short, stay on message. What you're creating now is a summary and an ending. End your speech in a style and mood that's congruent with the rest of what you've said. For example, you're not being fair to your listeners if you've kept them laughing throughout your speech, only to hit them with a stark recitation of doom at the end.

We've introduced a number of basic principles for effectively concluding a talk, so now let's quickly look at a structural outline for putting these principles into action.

Your conclusion starts when you signal that you're going to summarize what you've said so far. This is usually done with a phrase like "To sum up, here are the key points to remember . . ." Make this summary as concise as possible. The audience wants to make sure they know what you've said, but they also want to reach the end in a reasonable time.

Following the summary, many speakers like to move away from a procedural tone to appeal to the nobler motives of the audience. This is a good place for a quotation or a reference to an admirable and inspirational person. It's best to invoke someone whose name is already known to the audience. You link that individual to the task at hand. Phrases such as "In the best interests of our company . . ." or "For the sake of our nation and the world . . ." are appropriate. You can try to be more original, but time is a key factor in creating an effective conclusion. You may not have sufficient space in which to experiment. However, if you sense that the audience is truly on your side, you can share a brief, uplifting anecdote instead of just invoking a stock figure.

You should now throw down a challenge to the audience.

This should be a final call to action based on the argument you've made in your talk. It should also include a *reason* to act. The call to action should be clear and specific. Your audience should be left with no doubt about what you're asking of them. The reason to act should be based on what matters to them. Avoid phrases such as "I want you to . . ." Instead, for example, if your topic has been ways to increase work productivity, make it clear that your call to action represents an effective way to achieve that goal. Show them how your call to action serves their interests.

Make sure they understand what you expect of them, and what they should expect of themselves. It's hard to think of a better example of this than the quote from President Kennedy that we mentioned in a previous chapter: "Ask not what your country can do for you; ask what you can do for your country." Not many of us can be that eloquent, but the Kennedy quote is the gold standard to measure yourself by. The goal is to put the ball in the listeners' court in a convincing and emphatic way. If you can be poetic as well, so much the better.

While making this appeal, you have a great opportunity to reinforce it with an audio or visual component. The first choice would probably be a slide projection of something connected to the presentation. It could be an image showing the completed project, or a group picture of your team, or the text of a quote from someone that would appeal to the audience. An alternative is to distribute a symbol of some sort—a lapel pin, for example—to the audience. This can be distracting, but it's also an excellent takeaway that will remind people of what they've heard.

Finally, repeat the most important benefit in the fewest possible words. "We will see our goals realized." "Your income

will sharply increase." "You will fulfill your true potential."
Try to do this on a personal as well as an inspirational level.
Mention the names of people who can validate the benefit.
"As Susan and Barry have shown, meeting sales objectives
translates into higher pay." There's no need to overthink it.
The deepest needs of most people are relatively simple, and
foremost among them is the need to be admired by others.
When you offer that benefit to your audience, you're offering
them something that they deeply desire, even if they're not
completely aware of it themselves. What's more, you're offering them something that is actually within their reach. This
is the place to make that offer clear and to start them on that
path. When you've done that, the conclusion of your presentation is finished.

We've now reached the final pages of *Stand and Deliver*. Let's
quickly review the chapters that make up the book.

In chapter 1, we introduced key concepts of high impact
speaking, including total familiarity with your topic, diligent
planning, and extensive rehearsal. Beyond just understanding
your material, you need to *own* it.

Chapter 2 focused on the importance, first, of "knowing
thyself," and then on the ability of speakers to break down
the walls between themselves and their listeners. "Successful
communication depends upon how well a speaker can make
his talk a part of the listeners—and also the listeners a part of
the talk."

In chapter 3, we saw how stage fright is often not a fear of
failing, but of failing to be perfect. Once that unrealistic expectation is gone, so is the fear of speaking in public.

Chapter 4 dealt with the power of humor, and how even people who don't think of themselves as funny can access this valuable speaking tool. Humor is simply the easiest and best way to get an audience on your side, but it can also backfire if it's used incorrectly. Chapter 4 showed the differences between what's funny and what's not, and why all speakers should understand that there's nothing funnier than themselves.

The power of self-revelation was the topic of chapter 5. By sharing stories about themselves, especially stories from the heart, speakers can win not only the attention of an audience, but also affection and sometimes even love.

Chapter 6 dealt with the means for motivating an audience to action. What's required to get a listener to do more than just listen? We saw that sincerity on the part of the speaker is the true starting point. Being totally honest with an audience is the best gift we can give them, but we have to give it to ourselves first.

In chapter 7 we saw how to open a presentation strongly, how to "win the first minute." We also saw that a minute is actually an extravagant amount of time to give yourself. Speakers make an indelible impression in the first ten seconds—and it had better be a good one.

Chapters 8 and 9 were about the power of persuasion. What makes people set aside their doubts and inhibitions and take action based on a connection with another human being? The answer to that is what public speaking is all about. It's not necessarily simple, but it's within your grasp when you take these chapters to heart.

Chapter 10 introduced one of the most original and potent ideas of Dale Carnegie's work on personal development. The technique described in this chapter is simply the best way to move an audience to action when time is short. *Magic* is not a word to be used lightly, but what we learned in this chapter really is a Magic Formula for speaking success.

Finally, in chapter 11 we saw how a question-and-answer session can present both challenges and opportunities for public speakers. The key is to maintain poise, be respectful, and know how to avoid the traps that even well-intended listeners can sometimes set. That took us to our final chapter, in which the all-important conclusion of a talk has been our focus.

In closing, it's important to say a few words about success in general terms. This overview will benefit not only your career as a speaker, but also your life as a whole.

The stories of people achieving unusual success despite all manner of handicaps never fail to capture our attention. They're inspirational, but they're much more than that if we study them closely. The boy whose legs were terribly burned and who was told he'd be lucky to ever walk again becomes a champion track star. The woman blind and deaf from infancy becomes one of the most inspirational figures of the century. In this age of unprecedented immigration, we see examples of people who start off in this world with virtually nothing and within a surprisingly short time have become wonderfully successful. And we have many stories of men and women who were terrified of speaking in public but went on to become master speakers. Dale Carnegie training has helped many of them make this dramatic transformation.

What sets these people apart, people with vast handicaps such as not knowing the language, not knowing the right people, not having any money? What drives the boy with the burned legs who becomes a champion runner or a Helen Keller, blind and deaf, who becomes one of the most inspirational figures of our time? The answer, if fully understood, will bring you and me anything and everything we want, and it's deceptively simple.

The people we've cited in these pages had something the average person doesn't have. They had goals. They had a burning desire to succeed despite all obstacles and handicaps. They knew exactly what they wanted. They thought about it every day of their lives. It got them out of bed in the morning; it was the last thing they thought about at night. They had a vision of exactly what they wanted to do, and that vision carried them over every obstacle.

This vision, this dream, this goal, invisible to all the world except the person holding it, is responsible for perhaps every great advance and achievement of humankind. It's the underlying motive for just about everything we see about us. Everything worthwhile achieved by men and women is a dream come true, a goal reached. It's been truly said that what the mind can conceive and believe, it can achieve.

It's the fine building where before there was an empty lot or an old eyesore. It's the bridge spanning the bay. It's landing on the moon. And it's that little convenience store in midtown Manhattan. It's the lovely home on a tree-shaded street and the young person accepting the diploma. It's a low golf handicap and a position reached in the world of business. It's a certain income attained or amount of money invested. What the mind can conceive and believe, it can achieve.

Earl Nightingale expressed this more concisely than anyone else: "We become what we think about." When we're possessed by an exciting goal, we reach it. That's why it's been said, "Be choosy, therefore, of what you set your heart upon. For if you want it strongly enough, you'll get it."

In the developed world of North America and Europe, people are extremely fortunate. They *can* have pretty much whatever they want. The trouble is, they don't know what they want. Oh, they want little things. They want a new car; they get it. They want a new refrigerator; they get it. They want a new home and they get it. The system never fails for them, but they don't seem to understand that it is a system. Nor that if it'll work for a refrigerator or a new car, it will work for anything else they want very much.

Goals are the basis of any success. An excellent definition of success states, "Success is the progressive realization of a worthy goal." Or in some cases the pursuit of a worthy "ideal." Amazingly, this means that anyone who's on course toward the fulfillment of a goal is successful.

So success doesn't lie in the achievement of a goal, although that's what the world considers success. It's in the journey toward the goal. We're successful as long as we're working toward something we want to bring about in our lives. That's when the human being is at his or her best. That's what Cervantes meant when he wrote, "The road is better than the inn." We're at our best when we're climbing, thinking, planning, working. When we're on the road toward something we want to bring about.

The young person working to finish school is as successful as any other person on earth. The person working toward a particular position within his or her company is just as successful. The speaker who faces his or her first audience is already a major success. If you have a goal that you find worthy, a goal that fills you with joy at the thought of it, you'll reach it. But as you draw near and see that the goal will soon be achieved, begin to think ahead to the next goal you're going to set. It often happens that a writer halfway through a book will hit upon the idea for his next one and begin making notes or searching for a title even while he's finishing the current work. That's the way it should be.

It's estimated that about 5 percent of the population achieves unusual success. For the rest, average seems to be good enough. Most seem to just drift along, taking circumstances as they come, and perhaps hoping from time to time that things will get better.

The great Scottish writer Thomas Carlyle liked to compare human beings with ships. If we adopt this metaphor, the vast majority of men and women are like ships without rudders, subject to every shift of wind and tide. They're helplessly adrift, and while they fondly hope that they will one day drift into some rich and bustling port, for every narrow harbor entrance there are a thousand miles of rocky coastline. Their chances of drifting into port are a thousand to one against them. Their lives are like a lottery. Someone wins from time to time, but the odds are steeply stacked against them.

But the 5 percent who have taken the time and exercised the discipline to climb into the driver's seat of their lives, who've decided upon a challenging goal to reach and have fully committed themselves to reaching it, sail straight and far across the deep oceans of life, reaching one port after another and accomplishing more in just a few years than the rest accomplish in a lifetime.

If you visit a ship in port and ask the captain for his next port of call, he'll tell you in a single sentence. Even though the captain cannot see his port, his destination, for fully 99 percent of the voyage, he knows it's there. Barring an unforeseen and highly unlikely catastrophe, he'll reach it. If someone asks you for your next port of call, your goal, could you tell him? Is your goal clear and concise in your mind? Do you have it written down? It's a good idea. We need reminding, reinforcement. Getting a picture of your goal and sticking it to your bathroom mirror is an excellent idea. Thousands of successful people carry their goals written on a card in their wallet or purse.

When you ask people what they're working for, chances are they'll answer in vague generalities. They might say, "Oh, good health or happiness or lots of money." That's not good enough. Good health should be a universal goal. We all want that and do our best to achieve and maintain it. Happiness is a by-product of something else. Lots of money is much too vague. It might work, but it's better to choose a particular sum of money. The better, the clearer our goal is defined, the more real it becomes to us, and before long, the more attainable.

Success in any field comes from the *direction* in which you're moving. Children are happier on Christmas morning before opening their presents than they are Christmas afternoon. No matter how wonderful their presents may be, it's after Christmas. They'll enjoy their gifts, but they're often querulous and irritable Christmas afternoon. We're happier on our way out to dinner than we are on the way home. We're happier going on vacation than we are coming home from it. And we're happier moving toward our goals than even after they've been accomplished.

Life plays no favorites. Yet of one thing you may be sure: if your thinking is circular and chaotic, your life will reflect that chaos. But if your thinking is orderly and clear, if you have a goal that's important for you to reach, then reach it you will. One goal at a time. That's important. That's where most people unwittingly make their mistake. They don't concentrate on a single goal long enough to reach it before they're off on another track, then another, with the result that they achieve nothing. Nothing but confusion and excuses.

By thinking every morning, every night, and as many times during the day as you can about your exciting goal to become an accomplished public speaker, you are actually bringing that goal toward you. When you concentrate your thoughts on public speaking, it's like taking a river that's twisting and turning and meandering all over the countryside and putting it into a straight, smooth channel. Now it has power, direction, economy, speed.

So embrace your goal to become a master speaker. Insist upon it. Demand it of yourself. Connect with this goal every morning and night and as many times during the day as you can. By so doing, you will insinuate your goal into your subconscious mind. You'll see yourself as having already attained your goal. Do that every day without fail, and it will become a habit before you realize it. A habit that will take you from one success to another all the years of your life. For that is the secret of success, the key that will open the door to everything you will ever have or be.

Now that you've reached the end of the book, I hope you agree with the assertion we made at the outset: that *Stand and Deliver* is the most complete, powerful, and *practical* book ever created on the art and science of public speaking. We hope you'll use this book to achieve all your goals.

CASE STUDY:

Sports Talk

Sports movies have always featured motivational speeches, pep talks designed to inspire. The list of movie stars who have given these speeches is long and distinguished—Paul Newman in *Slap Shot*, Gene Hackman in *Hoosiers*, Denzel Washington in *Remember the Titans*, Al Pacino in *Any Given Sunday*, just to name a few. Theirs are certainly great speeches, but here are some examples of real people in sports and their real words.

Knute Rockne

Legendary Notre Dame football coach Knute Rockne was perhaps most famous for his inspirational "Win one for the Gipper" speech.

Rockne always said that George Gipp was the best all-around football player he ever coached. At twenty-five, Gipp contracted a fatal case of strep throat. When Rockne visited Gipp on his hospital deathbed, Gipp's last words to Rockne were:

"Sometime, Rock, when the team is up against it, when things are wrong and the breaks are beating the boys, tell them to go in there with all they've got and just win one for the Gipper. I don't know where I'll be then, but I'll know about it, and I'll be happy."

Rockne never forgot his friend's dying words, and eight years later he found his Fighting Irish in a tough game against their archrival, Army. Notre Dame was having a down year, having lost two of its first six games, and lots of people thought that Rockne had lost his magic. Before the game, Rockne gathered his players around him in the locker room and waited until there was total silence. Then he delivered a pep talk that would become one of the most famous motivational speeches in the history of football (or anywhere else).

Rockne began, "The day before he died, George Gipp asked me to wait until the situation seemed hopeless, then ask a Notre Dame team to go out and beat Army for him. This is the day, and you are the team."

Line coach Ed Healey later said, "There was no one in the room that wasn't crying. After Rockne finished speaking, there was a moment of silence, and then all of a sudden those players ran out of the locker room and almost tore the hinges off the door. In fact, some people say every team—and there were several—to whom Rockne said, 'You are that team!' reacted in exactly the same way!"

Lou Gehrig

New York Yankee first basemen Lou Gehrig was one of greatest baseball players ever to play to the sport. He was nicknamed the Iron Horse because of his remarkable record of playing in 2,130 consecutive games. That streak came to an end when, at thirty-six years old, Gehrig came down with a strange and crippling illness. Now known as ALS, the disease was originally called Lou Gehrig's disease. On July 4, 1939, at Yankee Stadium, Gehrig was honored in an emotional ceremony. When Gehrig addressed the crowd, he did not indulge in self-pity. Instead, he spoke about what a lucky man he was.

"Fans, for the past two weeks you have been reading about a bad break I got. Yet today I consider myself the luckiest man on the face of the earth. I have been in ballparks for seventeen years and have never received anything but kindness and encouragement from you fans. . . .

"So I close in saying that I might have had a tough break, but I have an awful lot to live for!"

Vince Lombardi

Legendary coach of the Green Bay Packers football team, Vince Lombardi delivered this pregame talk to his team before the 1968 Super Bowl. The Packers won, and it was be the last speech Lombardi gave to his team.

"Winning is not a sometime thing. It's an all-the-time thing. You don't win once in a while. You don't do things right once in a while. You do them right all the time."

The most famous quote attributed to Vince Lombardi—"Winning isn't everything, it's the only thing"—is something he never said. The speech you've just read is probably the basis for that famous misquote. The quote became so well-known that Vince Lombardi eventually gave up trying to explain that the words were not really his.

Herb Brooks

Coach of a ragtag collection of college hockey players who defeated the heavily favored Russians to win an Olympic gold medal, Herb Brooks gave this speech to his team before the game:

"Great moments are born from great opportunity. And that's what you have here, tonight, boys. That's what you've earned here tonight. One game. If we played 'em ten times, they might win nine. But not this game. Not tonight. Tonight, we skate with them. Tonight, we stay with them. And we shut them down because we can! Tonight, we are the greatest hockey team in the world."

Tim Tebow

All-American college quarterback Tim Tebow gave this speech after his Florida Gators lost a game to Mississippi:

"To the fans and everybody in Gator Nation, I'm sorry. . . . You will never see any player in the entire country play as hard as I will play the rest of the season. You will never see someone push the rest of the team as hard as I will push everybody the rest of the season. You will never see a team play harder than we will the rest of the season. God bless."

Joe Buck

Beloved baseball announcer Joe Buck was struggling with cancer when he made this speech in one of his final public appearances. It occurred on the day baseball resumed after the September 11 World Trade Center attack.

"I don't know about you, but as for me, the question has already been answered. Should we be here? Yes! Since this nation was founded under God more than two hundred years ago, we have been the bastion of freedom, the light which keeps the free world aglow.... We won't start, but we will end the fight. If we are involved, we shall be resolved to protect what we know is right.... As our fathers did before, we shall win this unwanted war, and our children will enjoy the future we'll be giving."

Jim Valvano

At the first ESPY Awards ceremony, North Carolina State basketball coach Jim Valvano, who had been diagnosed with bone cancer, gave this stirring speech:

"Three things we should do every day.... Number one is laugh. You should laugh every day. Number two is think. You should spend some time in thought. And number three is, you should have your emotions moved to tears, could be happiness or joy. But think about it. If you laugh, you think, and you cry, that's a full day. That's a heck of a day. You do that seven days a week, you're going to have something special. Cancer can take away all of my physical abilities. It cannot touch my mind, it cannot touch my heart, and it cannot touch my soul. And those three things are going to carry on forever. I thank you, and God bless you all."

Talk low, talk slow, and don't talk too much.

—John Wayne

Extemporaneous speaking should be practiced and cultivated.

—Abraham Lincoln

They may forget what you said, but they will never forget how you made them feel.

—Carl W. Buechner

Epilogue

It's a good idea to read this book (or any book) more than once. Sometimes, just because of human nature, important concepts get missed on a first reading. But if you don't have time to revisit the entire book, the summary that follows will connect you with the main points covered in *Stand and Deliver*.

First and foremost, speak on topics about which you feel passionately truthful. If you completely believe what you're saying, you'll automatically have a huge advantage over the vast majority of public speakers. If you only believe part of what you're saying, by all means emphasize that part as strongly as you can. Speak with conviction to the greatest possible extent. If you ever find yourself called upon to advocate a principle or a product about which you have real doubts, your long-term career will be best served if you find a way to avoid that obligation. It can become habit-forming, and the habit of dishonesty is definitely self-destructive.

Forcefully convey whatever emotions you really feel, but always be logical and well organized. If you fail to do this, your presentation may be compelling in the moment, but on their way through the parking lot, your audience won't remember what you said. They'll just remember how you said it, and it may not seem so hypnotic in retrospect. The material you present as a public speaker should include the same components as a written document you're preparing for publication. Your talk should logically progress from an introduction of both you and your primary thesis—to the body of your speech, including supporting anecdotal material that fosters a powerful connection with your listeners—to a conclusion that restates your thesis and calls upon the audience not just to hear you, but also to take action based on what they've heard.

Remember that effective public speaking depends on more than what you say. No one wants to watch you sitting down or standing still with your head down and reading from a prefabricated speech. How you look and how you move (or don't move) are central to your success or failure. Body language is important. Standing, walking, or moving about with appropriate hand gestures or facial expressions have been effective tools of public speaking since the time of the Roman Empire. Learn to use audiovisual aids or props for enhancement if appropriate and necessary. Master the use of presentation software such as PowerPoint well before your presentation—but make sure you don't come to depend on these technical innovations at the expense of developing your fundamental skills. Do not overwhelm your listeners with excessive use of animation, sound clips, or gaudy colors, which will only obscure you and your topic.

Don't read from notes for any extended period, but feel free to glance at notes from time to time. Speak clearly, neither too loud nor too soft. If you're going to be using a microphone, test it and get used to it before your presentation begins. Indeed, test everything: slide shows, computers with PowerPoint, recording devices, and anything else that might provide an unpleasant surprise during your talk. Rest assured, if your speaking career lasts for any length of time, unpleasant surprises are going to occur.

If something does go wrong, stay calm. Correct the problem yourself or let your support staff take care of it, then continue.

There's no need to apologize or make nervous jokes. A true sign of professionalism is the ability of a speaker to deftly negotiate a mishap. You may feel like crawling under a chair, but challenge yourself to keep your poise. If nothing else, you'll be able to look back on this as "the worst that can happen"—and know that you survived.

Maintain sincere eye contact with your audience. Do this one person at a time, using the three-second method. Try looking straight into the eyes of a person in the audience for three seconds, then move on to someone else. In this way you can have direct eye contact with a number of people among your listeners, while every now and then also scanning your gaze across the audience as a whole. Use eye contact to make everyone in your audience feel involved, both individually and collectively.

Learn to use silence as effectively as you use speech. Don't be afraid to pause during your presentation. Allow yourself and your audience a reasonable amount of time to reflect. Don't race through your presentation and leave your audience or yourself feeling physically out of breath and mentally disconnected.

Add humor whenever appropriate, but be careful not to overuse it. Keep your audience interested throughout your entire presentation. Remember that an interesting speech makes time fly, but a boring speech is always too long even if the actual time is the same.

If you're using handouts, have them distributed at the appropriate time. If your handouts will directly pertain to the content of your speech, inform the audience beforehand that you will be providing an outline of your presentation. By doing so, you'll prevent them from taking notes that might detract from their attention to what you're saying and how you're saying it.

Know when to stop talking, which may well be earlier than you might like. When practicing your speech at home, use a timer to determine not just the overall time of your speech, but also the amount of time required by specific sections. If one section is too long or too short, make an adjustment. To end your presentation, summarize your main points in the same way as you might in the conclusion of a paper written for publication. Close your talk with an interesting remark or an appropriate punch line. Leave your listeners with a positive impression and a sense of completion. Do not belabor your closing remarks. Thank your audience and sit down.

If there is a question-and-answer period, listen attentively to the questions, respond to them, and adjust your language if what you've been saying has obviously not connected with your listeners. Remember that communication is the key to a successful presentation. Remember too that the meaning of what you've said is the meaning that your listeners ascribe to it. Even if you feel they've misunderstood your speech, you must take responsibility for their misunderstanding.

Don't spend too much time on any one question. If you feel that time is running out, prepare the audience by saying, "I'll take one or two more questions." When you've done that, just thank the audience again. It's over. You did it.

And always be prepared for the unexpected!

About the Author

DALE CARNEGIE was born in 1888 in Missouri. He wrote his now renowned book *How to Win Friends and Influence People* in 1936—a milestone that cemented the rapid spread of his core values across the United States. During the 1950s, the foundations of Dale Carnegie Training® as it exists today began to take form. Dale Carnegie himself passed away soon after in 1955, leaving his legacy and set of core principles to be disseminated for decades to come.

Today, Dale Carnegie Training partners with middle-market and large corporations, as well as organizations, to produce measurable business results by improving the performance of employees with emphasis on leadership, sales, team-member engagement, customer service, presentations, process improvement, and other essential management skills. Recently identified by the *Wall Street Journal* as one of the top twenty-five high-performing franchises, Dale Carnegie Training has programs available in more than twenty-five languages throughout the entire United States and in more than eighty countries. Dale Carnegie includes as its clients four hundred of the Fortune 500 companies. Approximately 7 million people have experienced Dale Carnegie Training. For more information, please visit www.dalecarnegie.com.

Move from Ordinary to
EXTRAORDINARY

If you are serious about ...

- Earning more money
- Developing better relationships
- Having a more rewarding career
- Contributing more to those you care about
- Becoming the best you can be

Then log on to improveyourself.com

➡ **Use free mini courses** to quickly enhance your skills and increase your effectiveness in critical areas

➡ **Utilize life-assessment tools** to help measure the gap between where you are and where you want to be

➡ **Download free audio segments** from respected experts on wealth building, career success, health and wellness, communications, relationships, and much more

➡ **Take the test that assesses** your strengths and weaknesses — then provides you with a personal blueprint for reaching your goals

The best investment you can make is an investment in yourself

Created to help you become extraordinary

DALE CARNEGIE® TRAINING

ABOUT DALE CARNEGIE TRAINING®

Dale Carnegie partners with middle market and large corporations, as well as organizations, to produce measurable business results by improving the performance of employees with emphasis on:

- leadership
- sales
- customer service
- presentations
- team member engagement
- process improvement

Recently identified by *The Wall Street Journal* as one of the top 25 high-performing franchises, Dale Carnegie Training programs are available in more than 25 languages throughout the entire United States and in more than 80 countries.

Dale Carnegie's corporate specialists work with individuals, groups and organizations to design solutions that unleash your employees' potential, enabling your organization to reach the next level of performance. Dale Carnegie Training offers public courses, seminars and workshops, as well as in-house customized training, corporate assessments, online reinforcement and one-on-one coaching.

For more information, please visit www.dalecarnegie.com.